(From the original front cover flap)

About the Author

Ray E. Zinck is a veteran award-winning Canadian radio journalist. His documentary work has taken him to Africa, the High Arctic, under the Atlantic Ocean and to Europe, including war zones in Bosnia, Croatia and Cyprus.

With a business degree from Dalhousie University in Halifax, Ray lives in Yarmouth, Nova Scotia.

Cover photos, front: Joe Maloney's in 1944 (top); B-24 from the 464th Bomb Group during a bombing run (bottom).

Back cover: unknown crew of Maggie's Drawers, taken before Joe Maloney was assigned to her.

The FINAL FLIGHT *of* MAGGIE'S DRAWERS

A Story of Survival, Evasion and Escape

by Ray E. Zinck

TURNER PUBLISHING COMPANY

TURNER PUBLISHING COMPANY

Turner Publishing Company Staff:
Editor: Randy W. Baumgardner
Designer: Ina F. Morse

Copyright © 1998 Ray E. Zinck.
Publishing Rights: Turner Publishing Company
All rights reserved.

This book or any part thereof may not be
reproduced without the written consent of
Ray E. Zinck and Turner Publishing Company.

Library of Congress Catalog
Card Number: 90-60829
ISBN: 978-1-68162-401-3
Limited Edition.

TABLE OF CONTENTS

DEDICATION

Dedicated in loving memory to

Elsie Antionette (Schnare) Zinck
and
Victor Lloyd Zinck
My mother and father

and to

Gerald George Croft (1947-1964)
My friend

ACKNOWLEDGMENTS

I am grateful to many people in the preparation of this book. I only hope the following words of thanks and appreciation will serve as adequate recognition to all those who so kindly and generously offered their time, knowledge and patience.

First, a heartfelt thanks goes to the main subject of this book. Without Joe Maloney, this undertaking about such a compelling event would never have been possible. I am particularly grateful for his understanding and patience during the many occasions when I pestered him with my never-ending questions or tried to challenge his razor-sharp memory. Joe spared no time or effort in helping me to uncover many of his war time and family records, documents, letters, newspaper clippings and other countless pieces of information in the telling of this story. For this, I will always be thankful. I am also truly grateful for the never-ending confidence Joe and his wife, Flora Ann, placed in me in seeing this project through. This means as much as the friendship they have always shown me.

I benefited greatly from the keen editorial eye of my author friend, Joel Blau. He was instrumental in guiding and redefining my writing style and subject focus during the early stages of the manuscript. His keen insight, adept suggestions and astute criticism were invaluable.

Researching a story that reaches back to an event half a century ago required a lot of helping hands. Special thanks go to Archie DiFante at the Air Force Historical Research Agency, Maxwell Air Force Base, Alabama; Terry Jenkins and Owen Cooke at the Directorate of History, National Defense Headquarters, Ottawa; Professor Lawrence D. Stokes, History Department, Dalhousie University, Halifax, Nova Scotia; Professor James L. Stokesbury, History Department, Acadia University, Wolfville, Nova Scotia; Roland Stumpff of U.S. Veterans Affairs; and Stan Flentje and Henry Fasig Jr. of the 98th Bombardment Group.

Thanks also to several U.S. bomber crew veterans who contributed vital background material to this story: John Rucigay, Reinhold Schweitzer, Art Fleming, Ed O'Connor, Bill Crim, Bill Petty, Mike Meger, Paul Kuhns, Ray Kurner and Paul Haggerty. A special note of thanks to Eileen Streicher and Gladys Johnson for kindly offering information and documents on two of Joe's deceased crewmates. My gratitude also goes to Newbold Noyes Jr., war correspondent and former editor of the *Washington Star*.

There is a large debt owed to the scores of people I met and interviewed or who provided me with expert advice from overseas. From Slovenija in the former Yugoslavia, they include: Edi Selhaus, Janez Zeroyc, Stan Erjavec Sr. & Jr. , Stanko Kusljan, Franciska Sparovec, Anton &

Antonja Kos, Franc Brulc, Franc Planinc, Gorazd Planinc, Nilan Zagorc, Milan Zagorc, Jost Rolc, Dusan Kuret, Marija Klobucar, Franci Koncilija, Matija Zgajnar, Alenka Auersperger, as well as Ivo Matusic in Croatia and Dr. Ken Loutit in Morocco. In Austria, I would like to thank Rudolf Bistricky and Andrea Kofler. In England, my appreciation goes to Iain MacKenzie of the National Marine Museum in London.

Several individuals supplied me with documents, newspaper clippings and background research material, so, many thanks to Ana Brodarec, Cay & Harold Fields, Sam Tierney, Kay and Dick Munsen, Stefan Ferron, Trudy Parker, Arthur Thurston, Bruce Knowles and Tony & Mary Manion. My gratitude to Jim Harris for his technical assistance. Thanks also to Edi Selhaus for allowing me to include his wartime photo collection in this publication.

Several organizations also deserve mention for their outstanding research assistance: USAF Escape and Evasion Society, 98th Bomb Group, 15th Air Force Association, Slovene Partisan Hall of Records, Office of the Slovene Air Ministry, Ljubljana Museum of Modern History, Novo Mesto Archives and Museum, Ivo Matusic Air Museum of Matulji, Croatia, the National Archives and Library of Congress in Washington, D.C., Western Counties Regional Library of Yarmouth, Nova Scotia, and the Norfolk Historical Society.

Producing this book has taken its personal toll, especially during my sullen days of writer's block. Therefore my sincere appreciation goes to my wife, Louise, for her encouragement and understanding throughout the highs and lows of this project. Thanks to Lisa and Rhonda for never giving up on me. And, a tip of the hat to my very special friend, Cyprus.

INTRODUCTION

The man standing next to me had a faraway look in his eyes. We had been speaking for only a few minutes after meeting up by chance in the midst of a large, boisterous crowd. Wedgeport, a small fishing village hugging the rocky North Atlantic coast of Nova Scotia, was celebrating another summer festival. It was 1992, and, although we had been practically neighbors since he and his wife had retired to the eastern Canadian province in the early 1970s, I had known Joe Maloney for only a few months. As we exchanged small talk, the warm August night was ending on a high note with a dazzling fireworks show featuring a large cluster of flares lobbed high into the dark starry night. As the many points of light drifted back to the earth's embrace, small parachutes popped out, slowing their descent. It made for an impressive, albeit, eerie sight. This was the moment I first noticed Joe's troubled look.

He turned to me to say that the scene reminded him of the night the Germans were hunting him down during the war. His voice was flat and expressionless. His face a blank. It suddenly dawned on me that Joe was not in Nova Scotia at that moment. He was somewhere else — in some far off place, known only to him. He was probably having a flashback. I didn't know what to say. He never once even mentioned to me that he had ever been in the war. The more I stood there, the more his cryptic comment about the Germans rippled through me from head to toe. For the moment, I let it ride. Shrugging my shoulders, I filed the incident in the back of my mind, knowing this must be one of those bleak times of horrible memories for Joe, not unlike the war memories of many soldiers who I had always heard could never bring themselves to talk about it with anyone. Now was not the time to invade this man's private torment. But, I was hooked. I had to know more.

Let's jump ahead a couple of months. Joe and I happened to meet again. After exchanging some pleasantries, I decided to broach the subject that had been nagging me so since our earlier talk. Gently reminding him of the night of the fireworks show, I asked him to tell me more about the time the Germans were after him. He looked at me with penetrating eyes. He was sizing me up. No doubt he was not about to waste his time and energy, not to mention his emotional torment, on someone with only a casual interest in his story. Apparently satisfied with my sincerity, he began to talk, slowly at first, then, with greater confidence. His expression, however, remained matter of fact, as if he were recounting someone else's story. A way of removing himself from some painful memories, I assumed. The more he talked, the more I was impressed with his ability to recall even the smallest details. After all, it had been nearly a half a century ago. He continued to speak in measured, thoughtful tones, especially about the night the Germans used para-flares to try to catch him and his crew somewhere in occupied Yugoslavia. Toward the end of our conversation, Joe offered to lend me a stack of his personal papers: documents, letters, notes and newspaper clippings, from his war years. Of course I said yes. A few days later he dropped the package off to my house. I couldn't wait for him to leave.

As soon as he was out of the door, I dove into my prize. With reams of papers in one hand and a cup of hot coffee in the other, I began to read. I learned that two of his uncles had been killed in the Great War. There were lots of documents about his own war years-all dog-eared and original. A Missing in Action telegram to his mother in 1944 really caught my eye. I also found several neatly typed pages that meticulously outlined his military career from the time he was inducted until he was honorably discharged. I realized he was as good a writer as he was an oral historian. After several hours of intense reading, I sat back with the last scrap of paper in one hand and a cup of cold coffee in the other. I knew then that I had to write his story. The details of course were sketchy. But the broad outline was crystal clear in my mind. Essentially, it would tell the story of a young American airman going to war over Europe in a big Allied bomber as a tail gunner. The central theme would deal with the mission in which he and his crew were shot down, including the forces that shaped it, the actual plane crash and their subsequent evasion and dramatic escape from the enemy. The overall objective of the story, however, would be to tell more than just an isolated, historically factual, war adventure. It would attempt to interpret Joe's personal war experiences within the larger context of the American, British and Canadian bombing campaigns in World War II. It would also try to present Joe Maloney as more than just a young warrior, but rather, as an ordinary human being caught in the middle of a pivotal event of the 20th Century.

Then, it was down to the business of researching and writing. First, with Joe's fierce determination and tireless help, I attempted to locate his former crewmates, all nine of them, none of whom he had seen since the war. It was a tall order, but we had to try. We were to be disappointed, but not discouraged. After an exhaustive search that took more than a year, three of his former crewmembers could not be traced at all. It was as if the earth and time had swallowed them up without a trace. Sadly, we did discover that five of the men he had served with, half his bomber's crew, had died since the end of the war, some by accident, others by natural causes. We managed to track down only one of Joe's former buddies and he refused to talk about the war. Joe would be my only prime witness. As the only one left willing to talk, there was even more reason to get his memories down on paper. The window of opportunity on this World War II story was quickly closing.

Before Joe's story could even begin to take shape, I needed to know more about the air war itself over Europe. Without this backdrop, his story would have no context, no real meaning. The USAF Historical Research Agency at Maxwell Air Force Base in Alabama was a good starting point because it housed a wealth of information on the Allied bombing campaign during the war. The National Archives as well as the Library of Congress in Washington, DC, were also rich in research material, as were numerous veterans' groups and Air Force associations, both past and present. The pieces of this larger story slowly began to fall into place.

And what a story it was. On July 1, 1942, "Jarring Jenny" touched down at Prestwick, Scotland. The B-17 was the vanguard of the U.S. bomber fleet in Europe. The "Mighty 8th" had arrived in Great Britain. This in itself was a remarkable achievement, for only two years earlier the American Congress had cut an army request for 166 aircraft to 57, and refused to even entertain the notion of long-range bomber procurement, as this was considered "aggressive in its connotation." U.S. isolationism refused to go away even on the threshold of a world war. When Hitler invaded Poland in 1939, America quickly changed its tune.

Money was no object. $42 million went to developing heavy bombers, for which in 1938 the army has seen no real future. America's rising tide of industrial war production became an overnight flood. A mere year and a half before Joe Maloney was poised for action on a base in Italy, the USAAF had taken its first tentative step in the air war in Europe.

Although it met with early success, the ensuing American record did not bode well for Maloney and other crews by 1944. There was certainly no hint of trouble when, on August 17, 1942, a dozen Flying Fortresses took off from Polebrook, one of many American heavy bomber bases that had sprung up in East Anglia. Their target was the railway marshaling yards at Rouen in occupied France. For over three hours, those left behind, the ground crews, waited anxiously. Then, just before 1900 hours, a gaggle of twelve specks appeared. The USAAF had flown its first daylight mission and lived to tell about it.

By Fall, 1942, the B-24 had seen its first action in Europe when two dozen Liberators raided the heavy industries of Lille, France, that were contributing vitally to German armament and transport. One bomber did not come back while another ten were slightly damaged. The loss ration was acceptable. The rest of 1942 was a time of preparation, inconclusive combat and optimism for the USAAF. The average losses for both the B-17 and the B-24 remained at an impressive two percent, half that of the RAF. But no American bomber had yet flown to Germany. 1943 and 1944 would be very different, as Joe Maloney would ultimately learn.

Researching this story in overseas countries proved particularly difficult. Many of the documents I had sought through the mail from Joe's former enemies often arrived back months later written in German, Austrian or some other language. Translators had to be found. The Board of Trade in one particular Austrian town wanted to know why I was dredging up all this old information. Trust was difficult to earn, but, in the end, I received most of the information I needed.

Some of the overseas research could simply not be done by long distance. It required a visit to Yugoslavia, at least to the place where much of Joe's story took place. My 10 day visit there with Joe and his wife Flora Ann in 1993 was an eye opener. Language and culture were again a challenge but I learned a lot about what exactly happened to Joe and his crew in 1944.

One of the things a writer quickly realizes about a subject he's researching, is that there's often more than one story to tell. In this case, there were Joe's war experiences to be sure. But Joe and his crewmates were more than just young warriors. They were young men, ordinary young men, from ordinary backgrounds, thrust into extraordinary times and events. So, how did they cope? How did they manage to survive from day to day until the next mission and the next? Somehow, life, everyday life, had to go on, and, so it did, in a manner of speaking.

For instance, Joe used to pay a nine-year-old boy every week to clean his tent in Italy, the base of his bomber operations. The lad came from a very poor family and Joe saw this as a way of helping out, having gone through the Great Depression himself. Gino's mother did Joe's laundry once a week for a cake of GI soap. The boy also supplied him with fresh eggs once in a while. The exchange: two eggs for a pack of American cigarettes. It was barter. It was commerce. It was survival. It was life staring death in the face, the subtext of many war stories. Like Joe, Ray Kurner knew this lesson well. Assigned to Joe's squadron, he wrote some of his everyday experiences down years later. His insight reveals much about what these young flyers were all about.

"Truman Green and I put up the pyramid tent that we were to live in. Southern Italy can be cold in January, in fact, ice formed on the puddles. Our first priority was to winterize our tent. The Air Force provided kerosene, but not stoves to burn it in. Truman and I found a five-gallon round can with an intact lid. We scrounged a 10-foot length of concrete/asbestos pipe which we placed over the spout in the top of the can to serve as a chimney. From the aircraft junk yard, just north of our area, I salvaged some copper tubing. We cut a door in the can and a small hole through which we inserted the copper tubing. I coiled some of the tubing inside the can so the kerosene would preheat. The other end of the tubing was run outside to a five-gallon gas can which held the kerosene and which was siphoned to the stove. This heater worked great. The can would get cherry red and radiated heat throughout the tent. The only problem was that we had no way to turn it off, thus requiring someone to go outside and remove the tubing from the kerosene. Also, this required us to re-siphon the fuel each time we started the heater. I found a valve at the salvage yard and installed it in the line. Now we could turn off the fuel while inside the tent. We did not leave the heater on while we were sleeping because we were concerned about the possibility of fire. I do remember that when I turned the heater off at night, the tent became cold before I could get into my cot."

"Truman and I did some scrounging. The Italians were enlarging a maintenance hangar so we completed a midnight requisition and acquired enough four by four timbers to make a frame for the side walls of our tent."

"The squadron's intelligence officer and others lived in an English tent about 20 feet from ours. We noticed that they had a ground covering that looked like a carpet made of rope. We learned that it was a piece of landing mat. Another midnight requisition and we had our carpeting."

"My bed. We were issued Italian army cots and they were heavy. The canvass was very thick like a medical stretcher. The cross bar legs were cast iron and the side rails solid steel. It weighed at least 100 pounds. When I picked it up at supply, I balanced it on my shoulder and carried it to the tent."

Cunning, resourceful, inventive. These young fighting men knew how to survive in a hostile land, whether it was slogging it out on a military base somewhere in Italy in the middle of January, or marking time cooped up inside a noisy heavy bomber at 20,000 feet. But, no matter how they looked at life, there was still a war going on, a war that was slowly turning in the Allies' favor by 1943.

Confounded by General Georgi Konstantinovich Zhukov's massive Russian counteroffensive, Adolf Hitler's obstreperous Field Marshal Friedrich Paulus ignored orders to fight to the last man, and, instead told his weary troops to lay down their arms and surrender. It was noon, February 2, 1943. "Bararossa," the campaign that Hitler had so bombastically claimed would "decide the fate of Europe and the Third Reich," fell eerily silent over the blood red snow and smoking rubble of what was once Stalingrad. The German juggernaut had finally reached the high water mark of its military conquests.

This pivotal battle, Germany's failure to take Moscow, was a crucial turning point. By dividing and weakening his forces on two fronts, and unable to strike a peremptory victory in either one, Hitler was mortally wounded. If he had taken Moscow, and with it the rich resources of the Caucasus, most of his power could have been thrown against a faltering Allied attempt to secure a foothold in western Europe. The fight to finally defeat Germany could now proceed. It was no longer a matter of if, but rather, when.

The Allies were convinced that aerial bombing was the best road to final victory. But, they also knew that finishing off the enemy wouldn't be easy. And they were right. Only Hitler's maniacal obsession to win, or lose at all cost, kept the fight going.

By Spring 1943, the pace of the Allied air war was set by something called the Combined Bomber Offensive. The Americans and British had decided to coordinate their efforts. It would be a crucial test for the American bombers because the future of high altitude daylight precision bombing was at stake. To prove itself, the Americans insisted on pursuing a different air strategy from the RAF which turned to nighttime area bombing of German cities and towns. The Americans soon found themselves in deep trouble in the skies over Europe. By Summer 1943, their losses had mounted to a staggering 18.2 percent. An airman had only one in three chances of completing his tour of duty. Nevertheless, the United States Army Air Force (USAAF) pressed on with unbridled grit and determination.

By the time Joe and his crew had arrived on the scene to deliver their first payload in the opening months of 1944, the best efforts of the Allied air war were, quite simply, not good enough. America's air offensive was in imminent danger of total collapse. To make matters worse, by early 1944, German arms factories were humming with activity. Bombing seemed to spur the enemy to work harder. It was clear that Nazi air power had to be dealt a severe blow, or the great invasion of Europe in the spring could never begin. The Allies decided on a trial of strength with the Luftwaffe. It was time to do or die in the sanguinary skies over Europe.

The USAAF had more than 2,000 B-17 and B-24 heavy bombers to challenge Germany's aircraft production centers. This, they believed, would be the only way to rid the skies of enemy fighters. What enemy aircraft did make it to the armadas of heavy bombers, would be shot down by the new long-range escort, the P-51 Mustang, which had just arrived in the European theater to supplement the short-range Lockheed P-38 Lightning and the Republic P-47 Thunderbolt. The titanic struggle began in what became known as Big Week in late February 1944. Although American losses were relatively heavy, the Luftwaffe's losses were greater. More important, the Allies were finally able to start whittling down the Luftwaffe's reserve of young well-trained pilots. Men, not machines, were now Germany's most vexing problem. The Allied air war thus began a slow but a steady climb to recovery and ultimate victory. But, it would come at a high price. The enemy, with its big antiaircraft guns and para-flares, was still waiting to defend the Fatherland. Enter Joe Maloney and his bomber crew from the 15th Army Air Force in Italy.

It is not my purpose here to present a definitive military or tactical account of an event from World War II. Much has already been published on the subject of the air war, both in official academic form and in countless personal memoirs. This is one airman's unique story based largely on antidotal information and the recollections of those involved in this singular war experience. Every effort has been made to ensure accuracy in both fact and detail. Dialogue is reconstructed from the best recollections of those who were there. While the exact words used in direct quotations may be approximate, their context and meaning are a true representation of actual conversations. If there are errors or omissions in this book, they are mine alone.

August 1998, Yarmouth, Nova Scotia.

CHAPTER ONE

Silver Wings

The pilot's just a chauffeur,
It's his job to fly the plane.
But it's we who do the fighting,
though we may not get the fame.

A Gunner's Vow
Author Unknown

"You're in the army now." That was about the only coherent thought Joe Maloney could muster up in the soggy chill of that dark and dreary morning. Little wonder. February 5, 1943 was as cold and unforgiving as any New England winter could deliver. As he glanced up at the ponderous steel gates that shrouded the entrance to Fort Devens, Massachusetts, a mournful sigh welled up from deep inside his knotted gut. His quivering lips only made matters worse. Was it just the cold, or was he losing his nerve too? The piercing bark of a snarling drill sergeant put an end to his lingering doubt. Joe was as scared as hell, plain and simple.

Fort Devens, a sprawling compound of barracks, buildings and parade squares near Boston, was a staging area for raw army recruits from all over the U.S. northeast. Once in the grip of Fort Devens, the fresh faced inductees belonged to Uncle Sam, body and soul. First they were paraded around naked for every examination imaginable. Everyone, including Joe, was nervous and embarrassed. Jackie Mahoney was so tense that he couldn't even pee in a bottle. So, Joe did the job for him. After all, they had been best of friends for as long as either could remember.

More physicals, more shots and more than anyone would ever care to know about gonorrhea. That was the army's idea of the Welcome Wagon. It was anything but an auspicious start to ridding the world of the dirty Hun. But, a war was awaiting and Joe knew he had to get to it.

After several more days crammed full of aptitude tests, Joe demonstrated a natural ability for the air corps. His extraordinary knowledge of high school mathematics and drafting had finally paid off. He had easily grasped the concepts of trajectory

Left to right: Jackie Mahoney and Joe Maloney, January 1943 - 20 years old, Norfolk, CT. (Joe's best friend was killed in the war.)

and navigation, absolute essentials for any wanna-be flyboy. Things were beginning to look up. Better in the air than in some dirty foxhole, as far as Joe was concerned. And, to think, this all began on anything but a high note.

It was on another cold and miserable morning, only the month before, when Joe and 80 other young men, boys really, from all over northeastern Connecticut were whisked aboard two large busses parked in front of Station Place in downtown Norfolk. They were to meet a train 40 miles away in Hartford, the state capital, that would take them to Fort Devens. To his horror, Joe almost didn't even make it out of the starting gate.

Just as his bus rounded a sharp corner on the outskirts of Hartford, only minutes away from his destination, it skidded out of control on a patch of black ice and slammed head-on into a power pole. There was a lot of damage, but no one was hurt. Joe couldn't get over how quickly the driver had jumped up on his seat to keep his legs from being crushed by the impact. He wondered whether he would be as decisive when it came his turn to face the music.

After such a fitful start, Joe was never so glad in his life to see Hartford again. It was his old stomping ground, the place where he and his buddies used to drink some beer, cruise for chicks and raise a little hell. Now all he could do was stand there on the old wooden train platform and glance across the street to Bushnell Park, and beyond, to the familiar gold

15

dome perched atop the capital building. He would miss the comfort of his familiar surroundings.

Downhearted, Joe shuffled aboard the train and took a seat, deep in thought. The half day ride to Fort Devens was uneventful, giving him time to reflect on just how much his life was about to change forever. At this point he could only imagine what was out there. He was also uneasy about his decision to enlist, even though, deep down, he knew it had been the only thing to do.

By the beginning of 1943, Washington had lowered the age limit for the draft to 19 years of age. With his 20th birthday only months away, Joe knew he would be hearing from his local army board any day, so he volunteered in hopes of serving with some of his friends who had already been called up. However, the army didn't operate that way. Joe and his buddies would soon be scattered all over the United States for basic training.

Yet Joe would not regret his fateful decision on January 28, 1943 to report to Draft Board 31 at the Arcanum Building in Norfolk. After talking it over with his family, he knew what to do. Besides, he was ready, willing and able. As it had been at the time of the American Revolution, this small town in northwest Connecticut once again became a gathering place for those called into the service of their country. It offered up 191 of its best young men, including six brothers from the Kelley household who lived just down the lane from Joe's place.

As in the Great War, Norfolk was more prepared than most small towns for a good fight. The Norfolk Defense Council had already established the Air Raid Report Centre, a casualty station, victory gardens and rationing. And that was even before war had been declared. The folks of Norfolk were ready to do their duty, and so was Joe.

Within a week of arriving at Fort Devens, Joe had his first marching orders. He was to report to a troop train to ship out to boot camp, a trip, he was told, that would take about a week. As it turned out, the journey seemed more like a month because Joe had the unhappy experience of sharing his tiny pullman coach with his beefy friend Benny Serafini. There wasn't enough room for both of them to sleep at the same time. So, Benny took night KP and snoozed during the day, while Joe bunked down each night. Unfortunately for Joe, he never got all that much sleep. Benny insisted on bringing him food from the kitchen all hours of the night, every single night, making for a very fulfilling but exhausting trip. Joe certainly didn't need the extra calories. His six-foot frame already weighed in at a hefty 200 pounds.

There was no escape from his crowded quarters either. Whenever the train pulled into a station or a siding, and that was quite often during their roundabout route, heavily armed guards stood at every doorway with strict orders to shoot to kill anyone trying to get on or off. It was at times like these that Joe found it hard to tell which side the U.S. Army was really on. Joe and Benny were stuck with each other for the duration and that's all there was to it. When the train finally pulled into its last stop, nobody had a clue where they were. The military brass never divulged that sort of thing in advance because spies were everywhere. So the army said. Joe had already noticed a decided change in the weather from the previous few days. Word soon spread that they were in Miami Beach, Florida.

"Not bad for February," Joe muttered to himself, trying hard to shake the nightmare ice box that had greeted him at Fort Devens, as he and 120 other men huffed and puffed their way along Collins Avenue until they got to 42nd Street and the Ocean Spray Hotel. By 1943, The United States Air Corps had taken over most of the hotels in the area to house their raw recruits. It was three in the morning and Joe was dead tired.

Mopping a bead of sweat from his throbbing forehead, Joe squinted as he stepped inside the brightly lit hotel lobby, eager to catch 40 winks. Dawn would soon be breaking and he was looking forward to an easy first day of rest and relaxation. Again, the army had other ideas. After stowing his gear, Joe was ordered to report for roll call and breakfast. Without further ado, the gutwrenching grind of boot camp began. Joe needed no further reminders of "You're in the army now."

"A golf course, for Christ's sake," Joe still complains. "That's where they taught us to march!" Endless drills, on what were once lush-green fairways, lasted all day, every day, rain or shine. There were only two rules and God help the poor slob who broke either one they were constantly warned. Keep off the greens and out of the sand traps. But that was not all. When Joe wasn't slogging it out in full combat gear, he was fighting off coral snakes and scorpions whenever he tried to sit down for a minute. The food was even more of a challenge. Sunday chicken dinner invariably took top marks, a dish quickly renamed the "Seagull Special" for its wretched off-color texture and mangy taste.

There was some free time, but most of the men were so tired by the end of the day that all they wanted to do was sleep. It was their only escape from the constant drudgery. Through sheer grit and determination, Joe got through basic training and was officially accorded serial number 31-312-727. Now he was in the army for as long as Uncle Sam decided to keep him. It was March 30, 1943.

Miami Beach did offer the recruits at least one distraction during their stay. They always kept a sharp lookout for one particular but very elusive officer posted at another hotel just down the street from the Ocean Spray. Excitement filled the air whenever his name was mentioned because he was the outstanding leading man in American movies at the time. But, as luck would have it, Joe never got to meet Clark Gable. Not even a glimpse. Instead, all he came away with was the grand sum of $50 at the end of his six weeks. He figured he had earned every miserable penny of it. If there were any glory in war, he had yet to find it. Either way, it was time to move on.

Joe found it really hard to say good-bye to his pal Jackie Mahoney who was being posted to Flight Engineer School. With tears in their eyes they promised to get together first thing after the war. Meanwhile, Joe was off to air armory classes at Lowry Field near Denver, Colorado. It was early April by the time he came face to face with his strange new world. At this point, Joe was still uncertain about his future. He had failed his initial physicals because he was told he had an enlarged heart. Technically that meant he couldn't fly. In Denver he decided to try his luck one more time. It meant another physical, this time at the hands of a very gruff doctor. At the end of the examination, Joe was told to bend over and grab his ankles. He had to be checked for hemorrhoids he was informed. In the middle of the procedure, the doctor told Joe to cough. When he did so, the doctor burst out laughing. It was all a cruel joke. Joe was humiliated. But all was soon forgotten. In spite of the doctor's nasty sense of humor, Joe passed his physical. He would fly after all. Nevertheless, the road ahead would be long and bumpy.

First he had to learn how to strip down a heavy machine gun. Then he had to do it blindfolded. Later he was blindfolded and put inside a tiny closet with heavy gloves on to practice the same thing over and over again. It was the closest thing the army came to having a gun turret simulator. Joe learned everything there was to know about a machine gun.

Each day he absorbed more and more about the weapons of war, from light 30 calibre machine guns to the heavy twin 50s, to a vast array of bombs. From small incendiaries to the large demolition types, he soon knew them all, how they were made, fused, armed and exploded.

It was the heavy guns, the double 50s on the big bombers, that really intrigued Joe the most. There and then he decided he wanted to be an air gunner. Shipped back to Florida, this time to the Army Air Force Gunnery School at Tyndall Field outside Panama City, he was eager to learn anything and everything the army could throw at him. He had the confidence to become an air gunner, and perhaps even a good one at that.

Gunnery Class 43-34, the 34th class of 1943. That's where Joe found himself. From shooting clay pigeons with a shotgun in a standing position, he soon graduated to the bigger and better stuff. He was thrilled.

"I used to stand inside a waist-high metal ring on the back of a pickup truck that went like hell down a dirt road," he explains. "I had to shoot at clay decoys being flung from behind the bushes."

The trick was to catch a glimpse of the target just long enough to blast it to smithereens before the next one came along, and the one after that. It demanded nothing less than near perfect reflexes, flawless timing and nerves of steel. There was no such thing as a second chance in this school. Many of the men didn't make it. After surviving several weeks of this, Joe proved he had the right stuff. It was now time for the piece-de-resistance, practicing from the back of an AT-6 trainer. He was actually going to fly!

The single engine plane had an open canopy so student gunners could hone their skills standing up. After coaxing his bulky 200 pound frame into the tiny rear seat, Joe was raring to go. As the AT-6 wended its way a safe distance from shore, he couldn't wait to get into action.

"We were about 500 feet over the Gulf of Mexico when the pilot dipped his wings. That was my signal to start pumping bullets."

Taking aim at nothing in particular, Joe yelled "Take no prisoners," at the top of his lungs as he watched his rounds punch into the whitecaps below. A couple of minutes later the pilot dipped his wings again, the pre-arranged signal for him to stop shooting. Only Joe had been too busy to take notice. After getting off a few good rounds, his gun had jammed. Trying desperately to fix it, he had completely missed the second signal. A minute or so later he breathed a big sign of relief. His gun was okay. Just to make sure he pulled the trigger and let fly.

"The pilot nearly pitched me out of the cockpit with a real violent dive," Joe intones. "And when we got back to the base, I got an earful. I guess we were pretty close to shore when I let go with my last rounds."

Panama City nearly came under attack that day, he was told in no un-certain terms by a scowling instructor who was left wondering just whose side Joe was really on. It was anything but a great start for a gunner. But, after his rather mercurial debut, Joe eventually settled in at Tyndall Field, the largest of three gunnery schools in the United States at the time.

Each day brought a new adventure. Long cloth sacks, tethered by a cable to tow planes, soon replaced the white caps of the Gulf. Getting the knack of leading a target for the kill demanded his absolute best. Joe always seemed to measure up.

"It was never easy," he explains. "Just ask any of the poor pilots. Some-times the gunners were so far off, they would hit their own tow plane."

Lucky for Joe, or perhaps because he was in the top half of his class, his colored-coded bullets never seemed to make the wrong impression. He was a model student.

Tyndall Field wasn't all one big party in the wild blue yonder. Life on the ground was often anything but enjoyable for the young recruits. Even on scorching hot days, the gunners had to run and do calisthenics for hours on end when they weren't flying. The Summer of 1943 was particularly unforgiving in the panhandle of Florida and it made Joe's life down right miserable. "We were often so exhausted by the end of the day that we couldn't keep our food down," he complains. "But then who would want to? I mean, how much cow tongue, Spam and "shit on a shingle" (creamed sausages on toast) can a guy eat every day?" But, for all of his troubles, Joe did come away from Tyndall Field with his much coveted Silver Wings. As far as the army was concerned, his training was over. He was now a qualified air gunner with the United States Air Corps. He was another step closer to the war.

From Tyndall, it was back to Lowry Field for more specialized training before being assigned to an air crew. Joe was glad to be back in Lowry. Denver was different. Unlike Panama City that seemed to gouge the recruits whenever they ventured into town, he found the city nestled in the foothills of the Rocky Mountains full of warm western hospitality. Local families liked to open their homes to the itinerant soldiers for a meal or a weekend getaway. Joe was often invited along for fishing trips that would take him to some far off babbling mountain brook. He cherished his time away from the ubiquitous reminders of war. He embraced every opportunity to savor what he once knew and loved so far away in Norfolk. It was his only reminder of home. His only connection with sanity.

The chill of an early fall breeze greeted Joe as new orders were cut for his release from Lowry Field. The change in seasons reminded him of just how quickly time, not to mention his military career, was marching on. He was off to Biggs Field near El Paso, Texas for crew training. Another step closer to the front. Sitting in the shadow of Mount Franklin with its arresting 7,000 foot peaks towering over the Rio Grande River, El Paso was a dream come true for Joe. He immediately fell in love with the place. It was so different from the gently rolling hills of Connecticut. Biggs Field was just northeast of the city center and next to Fort Biggs, an army artillery base. But, as Joe would soon discover, Biggs Field could be a tricky place to land a heavy bomber as the mountain range lay just west of the landing strip. One night a bomber slammed into the mountain side on its final approach. There were no survivors. Biggs Field could be very unforgiving. It sent a cold shiver down Joe's spine. El Paso could also be very uncomfortable. Sandstorms, kicked up by fierce winds, often invaded this semi-desert region of Texas. Despite a quaint downtown built around a square with towering trees, antique benches, walkways and small ponds that were home to alligators, Joe took few good memories with him on his last day there. Except of course for his first taste of Fritos. And the scenery. Despite everything, El Paso was still a beautiful spot to this untravelled New Englander.

A newly promoted sergeant now making the princely sum of $78 a month, Joe was next sent to Grand Island, Nebraska, a transitional training base for those already qualified to join a regular combat crew. It was to be his last stop before going overseas. All he had left now was the wait.

Grand Island was a small town. It had a roller rink, a movie house, a few bars and, of course, the usual assortment of small restaurants. But after just one trip downtown, the airmen had little to do. Joe found out that the dry cleaning people in town always had an advance list of units for whom they could not accept any clothes because they were going to be shipped out within two days. So, everyday, Joe and his buddies made it their business to see if their clothes would be refused. In a town where there was nothing to do, it became a source of amusement. Sure enough, one day it happened, the dry cleaners turned them down. Two days later Joe had a new set of marching orders.

Circumstances at an air base in Tucson, Arizona had suddenly whipped Joe's timetable into overdrive. A bomber crew waiting for deployment there needed topping up after one of its gunners opted for flight school. Joe got the nod. His assignment: a heavy bomber. Something called a B-24 Liberator. He would be the newest member of its 10 man crew. He couldn't wait.

Although Joe was concerned about being a last minute replacement, in what he rightly figured would already be a tight-knit group, he felt right at home by the time the crew was posted to El Paso, Texas within the next couple of days. All air crews quickly became good friends, but Joe soon came to appreciate his new shipmates as much more. They were like brothers, willing to stick up for each other in any and all circumstances. They ate, drank, trained and played together with one objective: to become the best fighting machine they could be. Each man knew his own survival would depend on the others. Teamwork was not everything. It was the only thing.

Pilot Ed Brady was a quiet sort of guy who went into the service right out of high school. He always wanted to be in the military, so, when war broke out, he naturally jumped at the chance to become an air cadet, graduating a second lieutenant. Tall and slim with an athletic build, the Texan had a reputation for always putting his crew first.

Fred Streicher, the equally congenial co-pilot from Pittsburgh, told Joe he had enlisted on April 20, 1942, the day Hitler turned 53, a fact he was never allowed to forget. A party animal, Streicher was well liked by everyone in his crew. Whenever the food for the enlisted men got unbearable, and that was quite often, Streicher would always make sure they could sneak into the officer's mess for some decent grub. That's the kind of guy he was. The other officers didn't like this breach of protocol, but they never openly challenged him.

Joe quickly pegged Clark Fetterman as the mother hen of the group. The bombardier, also from Pittsburgh, was a stickler for detail and a real gentleman.

"It's amazing the little things you remember about somebody," says Joe. "With Clark it was a photo he always kept with him-but not just any photo. Seems one day he wrote to Shirley Temple, the movie star, and she wrote back. Her photo was his good luck charm."

The most reserved officer in the bunch was William Birchfield. Never one for many words, the navigator pretty much stuck to himself. But the Texan knew his job and that's all that mattered as far as Joe was concerned.

One of the crewmen who really impressed Joe right from the start was Flight Engineer Clarence Jensen, a native of Fresno, California. There was nothing, it seemed, that this man didn't know and couldn't do when it came to an airplane. Jenson actually ended up flying some of their training missions so Brady and Streicher could sleep off a hard night of partying at the back of the plane. All of 24 years of age, Staff Sergeant Jensen was the old man of the bunch.

The crew also had its share of raucous characters, John Reilly among them. Raised in a large Irish-Catholic family in Arlington, Virginia, the radio-operator, who doubled as top turret gunner, was always quick with a joke and even quicker with a poke in the ribs for anyone foolish enough to stand within his reach. He and Joe quickly became close friends, something that would serve them well later on.

The rest of the crew, all enlisted men, held the rank of sergeant. At 5'2" and 120 pounds, Art Fleming was head and shoulders below the rest when it came to physical size. A good thing. The native of Clairton, Pennsylvania was just the right size to squeeze into the ball turret, the tiny glass bubble slung beneath the fuselage.

Joe liked to keep his distance from William Kollar because he was the kind of guy who was always pushing his luck and usually losing. The waist gunner, from Lowell, Michigan, was a consummate gambler. Always broke by the end of every payday, he had an uncontrollable urge to shoot the dice. The way he tempted fate simply amazed, but more often than not, disgusted everybody around him.

Joe quickly pegged Waldo Akers, the other waist gunner, as the unmitigated scamp of the bunch. It never seemed to fail that, the bigger the mess he got into, the more he rose to the occasion. Joe recalls one such incident with a rueful smile.

"We had all just been issued 45 caliber service pistols, so Waldo and I decided to draw some ammunition for target practice," he says. "Our little stunt almost got me kicked out of the Army."

No sooner had they stepped onto the range when they were confronted by a very angry field commander, a general no less. Joe nearly died. "He chewed us out for being in flight fatigues off the flight line," he remembers. "I was so mortified I couldn't say a word. I thought we were going to be court-martialed right then and there."

Without missing a beat, Akers decided to turn on the charm. As usual he knew exactly what to say. "Sir, we just flew in and we didn't know the field regulations," he offered by way of an explanation. Joe knew it was a bold faced lie. Now they would be court-martialed for breaking regulations *and* lying to a superior officer. But Akers' cool pomposity worked as usual. "Very well then," came the almost meek reply, as the jeep sped off.

The newest member of the crew was assigned the tail turret. Joe was also the armorer gunner, which meant he was responsible for every piece of ordnance on the ship. If a problem arose during a mission, it would be his job, and his job alone, to fix it. If a bomb got hung up on the racks, he would have to be the one to pry it loose. It meant going out on a long, narrow catwalk in the middle of the open bomb bay with nothing more than 25,000 feet of howling wind beneath his feet. He would also have to do it without a parachute. The passageway was too narrow for a bulky chest pack. And, to make matters worse, a snagged bomb could only be pried loose with a screw driver, leaving Joe to hang on for dear life with only one hand. He didn't look forward to this part of the job.

Joe and his crewmates had little to do while they waited for their orders to be sent overseas. Just before that fateful day, they were granted a week's furlough to go home. Joe hungrily snatched it, knowing it might be his last hurrah. Back in Norfolk his leave quickly passed. He was just as glad. It just didn't seem like home anymore, especially with all his friends gone. He missed Jackie Mahoney more than ever.

Back in Tucson this time, Joe rejoined his crew for another waiting game. By now he had chalked up a total of 35 hours and 55 minutes of intense flying time. He was as prepared as he was ever going to be. So was his B-24. Ed Brady, Fred Streicher and a couple of the other officers had already made sure of that.

One day they decided to take their ship up for a spin, just to see what she could do. They figured the experience might come in handy. Flying at the maximum altitude of 30,000 feet, Brady nosed the B-24 over into a steep dive. It almost proved fatal. The bomber went straight down 19,000 feet before Brady and Streicher, pulling with all their might on the yoke, managed to move the aerilons and elevators enough to level out. Everything that wasn't bolted down flew into the air during their zero-gravity plunge. But, they managed to pull off their first real test and live to brag about it. It had to count for something, they hoped.

This was not the end of the crew's adventures. A few days before their scheduled departure, a big fist fight broke out among some soldiers in town. The incident was serious enough that Joe's crew almost didn't get to ship out as a unit. "I stayed out of it," says Joe. "But some of the guys in my crew mixed it up real good with some army types after a night of drinking. They were all promptly arrested."

Court-martial orders were drawn up, but, Major H.D. Pomeroy, the escort officer for Joe's crew, understood the excesses of youth especially at a time like this. The seasoned officer assigned to take the airmen overseas to their combat units and then return to the States for another batch of young, untried flyers, stepped in to save the day. The major came up with a simple but effective solution. He neatly folded up the court-martial orders and pushed them to the back of a pigeon hole behind his desk, stuffing a few letters out in front for good measure. "We'll be a long time gone before anybody finds these," he said. He was right. On November 29, 1943, Joe and his crew finally got their marching orders. Joe was promoted to staff sergeant, a routine procedure for enlisted men leaving for the front.

A few days later, the Pomeroy Provisional Group arrived at its point of departure, the U.S. Naval Base in Newport News, Virginia. As the bump and grind of his troop train ground to a final halt at the station, Joe accepted the inescapable fact that his destiny awaited, just as it had for an earlier generation of Maloneys in another war.

CHAPTER TWO

Ab Initio

A Swell Lot Of Christians We Are
> *Frank Ferguson, Canadian Expeditionary Forces*
> *April 8, 1917*

August 4, 1914. A spark ignites Europe's powder keg, plunging the world into war. On that day the humorless British Foreign Secretary, Sir Edward Grey, stood at the window of his Whitehall office in London deeply absorbed in conversation with a close friend. "The lamps are going out all over Europe; we shall not see them lit again in our lifetime," he observed prophetically. Within a matter of a few short months, what had been popularly touted as a "war of rapid movement" that would be over by Christmas, descended into a nightmare of battlefield gridlock. It marked the genesis of four long years of deadly attrition along the Western Front from the North Sea to neutral Switzerland, taking with it millions of lives.

Although the American Civil War, and the Franco-Prussian and Russo-Japanese Wars of the preceding century had clearly underscored the significance of advances in firepower, the General Staff in 1914 failed to grasp the implications of their own industrial age war machines. A hideous pattern soon developed whereby each side invited a holocaust upon themselves in the muddy, rat infested trenches of France and Belgium. There was no let-up to the constant blood letting. More and more countries were faced with the inevitable need to throw more and more men and resources into the quagmire.

A staunch foreign policy of non-participation, steeped in its frontier

Joe in full combat gear just before his posting overseas, 20 years old. Salt Lake City, 1943.

heritage, kept the United States out of the apocalyptic sacrifices of Europe, at least at first. But, in doing so the country ultimately faced two intractable problems. Many Americans were of European stock so they naturally took sides. The United States was also a rich source of war materiel, which each side tried to keep the other from getting. The country was therefore caught between two fires. Ever increasing attacks by German submarines against neutral shipping, particularly after January 1917, inevitability nudged America towards war. A few months later, the United States had had enough. Its declaration of war against Germany, and later, Austria-Hungary, marked its brief but bloody involvement in the carnage of European trench warfare.

The United States had been meagerly prepared in April 1917, with no one, in or out of the army, having any practical training or experience. It is little wonder that, after arriving in France, General John Pershing wisely notified the War Department to discontinue shipments of bathtubs, bookcases, lawn mowers and spittoons. He was astute enough to quickly realize he was facing a very different kind of war.

As the fighting entered its final stages, American losses were relatively light compared to the more seasoned nations. This of course was of small comfort to the grieving families back home. Despite its late entry into the war, few American communities were spared the horrors of the Great War.

On March 17, 1918, 44 "boys" of Company M, 102nd Regiment, were trapped by a surprise enemy barrage in northern France. Hailing from the Norfolk, Connecticut area, the squad of young untested troops on the Chemin des Dames front weathered some heavy artillery fire and gas attacks.

It took two full weeks for word from the front to finally reach home. Twenty-two year old Private John Bouchet of Norfolk, who had signed up with the 26th Division of the New England National Guard only seven months earlier, had been severely wounded. A few weeks later the army also dutifully informed the Bouchet family that their only other son had succumbed to gas poisoning as a result of the same skirmish. As a cook in a front line field kitchen, Paul Bouchet likely never even saw the mustard gas coming.

26

Although the Hague Convention prohibited the use of such weapons, the Germans launched the first large-scale gas attack in early 1915. Five months later the British reciprocated, and, from then on, both sides were off to the races. One veteran, a Canadian, remembers the horrors of being gassed.

Clifford Earle of Yarmouth, Nova Scotia, says his brush with "Yellow Cross," so called because of the German shell markings, came one day when he and a couple of other soldiers were caught in a standoff with a small band of enemy soldiers.

Detecting a whiff of mustard gas in the wind, Earle ordered his two buddies to don their masks. But, after a few minutes, they had to pull them off their eyes in order to see. When darkness came, the Germans retreated. Earle and his men subsequently returned to their rear lines. The next morning all three of them woke up blind as bats. It took a full week for them to get their sight back.

Earle, who survived several more gas attacks, always found mustard gas to be virtually undetectable because gas and smoke shells were a common mix in most barrages. Unfortunately, men like Paul Bouchet were simply unaware of the danger more often than not and therefore paid the ultimate price.

Damage to the 21-year-old's lungs resulted in a rapid loss of fluid from his blood, causing severe edema and a slow agonizing death. On that same fateful day, Sergeant Joseph Roberts of Norfolk was also killed. His brother Lester, a motorcycle dispatcher with the same outfit, managed to survive.

Memorial Green, a triangular spit of land rising up from the meandering Blackberry River, stands as a mute tribute to Norfolk's fallen sons. The Roberts-Bouchet Branch of the American Legion was named in honor of the town's first tragic losses in the Great War. Although Joseph Roberts and Paul Bouchet would never know it, they would not be the last of their clan to do battle in some far off land. Two decades later, there would be another war and another call to arms in Norfolk The name Joe Maloney would be added to the list.

A quarter of a century later, On December 7, 1943, hundreds of troops, fresh from training bases all across the United States shuffled up the gangplank of a British troopship waiting at the mouth of the James River at Newport News, Virginia. As the brash strains of a colorful military band sliced through the somber mid-day fog, Joe Maloney was about to join the new Allied drive to kick the living hell out of the Axis' death rattle. At the very least, he was hoping to play a part in helping to seal the fate of the 1,000 year Reich, as the leather straps of his heavy battle gear burrowed deep into his shoulders and back.

From the barren snows of Stalingrad to the burning sands of North Africa, Adolf Hitler had already lost the initiative and had begun to witness the unrelenting hemorrhaging of his once mighty war machine. By early 1942 the British had already carried out its first 1,000 bomber raid over Germany, while more and more high altitude raids were being dished out by the heavy bombers of the USAAF. The enemy fought back with speedy fighters and improved ground defenses, but still the bombers came, the British by night and the Americans by day.

Soon after weighing anchor at about 3 o'clock, Joe quickly realized that getting to the front would be anything but an event to remember. It was a cool day with a slight breeze from the west. The ocean was relatively calm as their ship picked up steam to about 17 knots in a southeasterly direction. So far so good. However, conditions above deck, at least for the first couple of days, belied a much bleaker situation below. The Royal Mail Liner "Andes," converted to an Allied troop transport, was cramped to say the least. Even a swimming pool on the foreword deck was filled to the top with military gear, not water. Built in 1939 to accommodate just over a 1,000 passengers and crew, the "Andes" had no fewer than 500 airmen and 5,000 infantrymen aboard for this crossing.

From greasy English food, to fowl weather, to a submarine scare, it would be an adventure Joe would never forget. The rough Atlantic soon took an immediate and terrible toll on the foot soldiers in particular. Most of them became horribly seasick. The airmen, used to the ups and downs of their trade, fared somewhat better. But no one could escape the harsh daily regiment of greasy boiled potatoes, cabbage, mutton and rancid sausages that looked and tasted more like oil-soaked sawdust, all served up with weak tea with the milk already in it. Even the beans and wieners had the consistency of brown mush.

The sickly sweet smell of the food and the constant rolling of the ship were a lethal combination even for those with cast iron stomachs. After giving it his best, Joe turned up his offended nose and decided to buy sardines and crackers from the ship's canteen for the rest of the trip. It was better than starving to death, but it turned him off sardines for the rest of his life. Little wonder.

Even sleep offered no reprive from the constant misery. The five and a half thousand men had to bunk below deck in a maze of hammocks stacked like cordwood. Once in bed, no one ever got out until morning. Pity the poor guy who had to go to the head in the middle of the night. That's what a helmet was for. A rhythm of farting and belching echoed through the cold dark bowels of the ship night after night. Personal hygiene went by the boards as the men never once got to change out of their sweat and vomit stained woolen uniforms.

For all of its appalling conditions, the "Andes" had at least one redeeming quality. She was fast. In fact, fast enough to sail without the usual protection of a convoy. Half way across the Atlantic that advantage paid off in a big way. There was a sub alert. Everybody was ordered up on deck with their Mae Wests in tow. For a tense filled hour they stood by as the "Andes" made a run for it. Finally the all clear bell sounded.

Had disaster struck, few of the men would have had any chance of surviving the cold Atlantic. Besides, the "Andes" didn't even carry enough lifeboats. That was simply impossible with 5,500 souls in her hold. The scare weighted heavily on Joe's mind. Many of the men refused to go below for the rest of the trip, preferring to take their chances in the freezing salt spray of the open deck.

There wasn't much to do on the ship. Gambling filled up much of the time. A lot of money changed hands. A few fist fights broke out among the troops, probably the result of the close living quarters.

Eight miserable days out of Newport News, the tormented human cargo finally arrived at its destination in North Africa-Casablanca, French Morocco to be exact. On the morning of December 15, Joe wobbled down the gangplank and stepped ashore. He nearly puked his guts out. His head wouldn't stop rocking with the motion of the ship. He wondered how any war could be any worse than the hell he had just been through. Grown men fell on their knees and kissed the ground. That's how glad they were to be off that cursed ship.

Eleven months earlier, Casablanca had been the site of a major conference between the Big Two, United States President Franklin Roosevelt and British Prime Minister Winston Churchill. It was in this French occupied city that a crucial decision had been reached over how the war would end. The Casablanca Conference concluded that the Allies would exact nothing less than total unconditional surrender from the Axis. It would be all out war until the bitter end.

The Allied objective was to be achieved, in part, through an all out bombing campaign against the enemy's strategic military targets. This is where the American high altitude daytime bombing campaign would finally pay off. At least that was the grand plan as Joe's crew began to settle into its new home.

Casablanca was an eye opener for the uninitiated Yankees. Their welcome was a horde of dirty faced kids lined up along the route to their camp. Children, as young as four or five, pleaded with outstretched hands for gum, candy, cigarettes, anything the Americans might spare. The older Arab boys yelled at the GIs, offering to let them have sex with their virgin sisters for a quarter. The kids knew all the right words, words they had obviously picked up from the GIs who had come before.

With modest New Englander roots, Joe was a little more than ashamed and embarrassed to hear such stuff come from the mouths of such babes. "Son-of-a-bitch" and "bastard" were among the favorites. As his truck lumbered towards the east, Joe came to the conclusion that either the young

Moroccans were a quick study in the seamier side of American culture, or they simply didn't understand what they were saying. He preferred to believe the latter, although he really knew better.

The army camp, a city of GI pyramid tents, was stuck in a sand dune in the middle of nowhere about five miles from the outskirts of Casablanca. Camp Don B. Passage was hot, filthy and very trying on the nerves. Never a night went by without something happening to keep the young airmen on constant edge.

"I would often wake up in the middle of the night to find somebody's arm poking through my tent flap," remembers Joe. "They would steal anything we didn't have nailed down. We would capture some of them but it never did any good. After letting them go with a warning, they would be right back at it the very next night."

The climate also became a problem. Casablanca was warm during the day but cold and very damp at night, a condition that soon played hell with the urinary systems of more than a few of the men. Joe was kept awake many a night by his incessant need to go to the latrine. If it wasn't one thing it was another.

Even the Allied cemetery in Casablanca needed 24 hour armed guards, especially after a fresh burial. Grave robbing was commonplace because of the poverty. Gold fillings played a big part in the black market. However, not all of the nefarious deeds were one sided. One night, Fred Streicher and Waldo Akers decided to steal some horses from a nearby village to go to the nearest kasbah, where some Arab women were being housed.

"I guess they wanted to say hello," Joe chuckles. "But what they got was a lot more than they had bargained for."

World War III nearly broke out when the two airmen were jumped from behind by a band of burly men assigned to guard the compound and the women inside. Streicher and Akers barely made it back to camp alive with the angry mob in hot pursuit. They were lucky that their own guards didn't shoot them on sight after they came charging through the front gates at full gallop in the dark. As usual, Waldo Akers had managed to pull another rabbit out of his hat.

As luck would have it, bad luck in this case, Joe's 500-strong air corps was stuck in the middle of a huge U.S. Infantry camp which made for a lot of rivalry and some very hard feelings. To make matters even worse, Camp Don B. Passage was right next door to a U.S. Army disciplinary prison camp for G.I.s who had gone "wrong" during the invasion of North Africa. The American prisoners stood accused of dissertion, cowardess and insubordination among other military crimes.

Everyday Joe watched with amusement as the prisoners were marched out of their compound, complete with military music. Starting at 6 a.m., the men were herded down a road led by a jeep with a guard at a mounted machine gun. Another jeep, similarly equipped, followed behind. One other thing. If the prisoners failed to pass inspection before breakfast, they didn't eat for the rest of the day. And these were Americans! It instilled in Joe a whole new appreciation for army authority. But it galled Ed Brady to no end when the army regulars tried to extent their authority over his airmen.

"In three and a half years in the army I have never met a more chicken shit collection than this outfit," he wrote home bitterly.

In the same brutally frank note to his sister, Brady didn't stop there. He cursed the fact that his men were forced to do three hour hikes every morning before breakfast while the infantry boys were allowed to sleep in like "pampered babies."

"Since they had more rank and authority, we had to take it," he added. "The only real reason seems to be the fact that we are Air Force and they didn't like us."

But life was tough all around. Army or air, every man had to make do with only one helmet full of water a day, no matter how hot it got. And that one helmet full had to do for washing, shaving, and brushing teeth. There were no showers to fight the sticky heat, not even for the officers. Everybody suffered equally when it came to the lack of water.

Although the days were long and tedious, Casablanca was not entirely without its moments. A favorite meeting place in the city for those off duty was *Le Rustque Bar.* The favorite beverage was Grenache wine, drunk by the bucket full of course. From a tower at city hall, Joe could even see the French fleet in the harbor. Some of its officers had been part of the Vichy regime and could not be trusted.

But the camp's latrine was the real source of daily amusement. Situated next to a busy dirt road, it was little more than a bunch of planks strung over an open trench. The only thing that separated this public convenience from the bemused smiles of the locals making their way to market each morning, was a wire fence.

"We used to sit there and watch the peasants walk by wearing our stolen barracks bags," says Joe. "They would use the drawstrings as belts and let their legs dangle out of two holes they had cut out of the bottom. They always looked very pleased with their new pants. Some of the names and serial numbers were still stamped on the canvas for us to see."

But then the Americans got some real strange looks back. Sitting on those hard planks with their bare butts hanging out every day must have been quite a sight to those passing by. Despite such risible episodes, Joe and his crewmates never warmed up to Casablanca. Ed Brady summed it up in another letter to home.

"In North Africa there seems to be a polyglot of races and refugees all intent on robbing, swindling, cheating or begging from you. For the right amount of money you can buy anything."

The open air markets of Casablanca offered Joe and the others a brief escape from the war. There were lots of things for them to buy and send home to mother or a sweetheart. Brass vases, pictures and candle holders were hot little items. Joe was impressed with the vibrant colors of the women's gowns and the quality of the leather goods on display at every corner. Even during war, it seemed to him, life went on.

On returning to camp one evening, Joe noticed about two dozen men lined up outside a chemical warfare tent near the gate. An officer by the name of Ray Kurner also happened to notice the same thing and found it curious because it was such an odd time for a gas mask drill. Only later did they learn that this was no drill. Two Arab women were in the building selling there wares while their customers lined up outside.

Joe's crew was getting more and more restless. To compound matters, there were no planes around to keep their skills sharp. This was like a death sentence. Besides, they made more money when they were flying. They were no better off than the sand fleas that shared their tent space. But, by the first part of the new year, they finally got the break they had been looking for. Their brief albeit memorable stopover in Casablanca came to an abrupt end with another set of marching orders.

By early 1943, Sicily, the vital steppingstone to Italy, had already fallen to the Allies. Coupled with a crushing defeat of its army in North Africa, the loss of Libya, and the toppling of dictator Benito Mussolini, Italy was now primed for unconditional surrender.

By September 1943, the British 8th Army had captured Foggia, the biggest airbase in southern Italy. And, the U.S. Fifth Army had moved to a point just south of Cassino, half way between Naples and Rome a short time later. Although the Anglo-American ground campaign continued to schlep northward against a fierce German rearguard action, the Allies at last had a base on the Continent from which to penetrate more deeply into the soft underbelly of Hitler's Occupied Europe. Joe's crew eagerly scrambled out of Africa to a newly captured base on the heel of Italy, only to be disappointed again.

"Manduria was nothing but a mud hole," Joe quickly realized. "It was so bad that our landing strip had to be covered with steel mats just to handle the extra load of our heavy bombers. It was an accident waiting to happen."

When weather and runway conditions permitted, and that wasn't very often, a squadron of heavy bombers marked time by honing their skills in close formation flying, strafing and bomb aiming. At least Joe and his crew now had something to do once in a while.

But, whenever somebody tried to take off or land, a heavy gloom hung over the base. From the dry wind-blown sands of Africa to the wet sticky mud of Italy, there was to be no happy compromise. Joe worried about the way the steel mats always tended to form hills and valleys on top of the soft mud.

B-24 crash that killed four, including Col. William E. Karnes. Manduria, Italy - January 1944.

The washboard surface had the maddening tendency of hurling the bombers into the air during takeoff before they were actually airborne. On January 13, 1944, only days after Joe had arrived in Manduria, disaster struck. Joe was standing in the waist window of his bomber, only a couple of hundred feet off the runway, when his worst nightmare unfolded right in front of his eyes.

"A B-24 was nearly at the end of its takeoff roll, bouncing violently as usual," he recalls. "The pilot retracted the landing gear thinking he was airborne but he wasn't. Seconds later he tried to put his wheels back down, but it was too late."

A thunderous screech of metal against metal erupted as airplane and runway collided. The main landing gear on only one side of the bomber had locked into position. The nose gear had also failed to lock. The B-24 did a complete headstand as it careened down the runway leaving a spectacular train of sparks in its wake. The plane's undercarriage sheared away from the rest of the fuselage from the nose turret to the wing section.

Joe jumped from his waist window and sprinted across the muddy field to see if he could help. Fortunately there was no fire. But there was almost total devastation. Every prop had been ripped from their mounts and engine number three was still running at full throttle.

With tons of aviation fuel seeping all over the runway, Joe was scared the overheated motor might set off a huge explosion. He didn't dare go any closer. All he could do was stand by and watch as the medics risked their lives pulling the mangled bodies from their twisted metal coffin. Joe had yet to see any combat and already his friends were dying. It was a sobering day to say the least.

Among those who perished that day was Joe's base commander, Colonel William E. Karnes. He had been set to teach his young charges the ins and outs of combat formation flying later that same day. The co-pilot, bombardier, navigator and radio operator, all good men, also lost their lives. Luckily, there was only a skeleton crew aboard. The airmen were buried with full military honors at the U.S. military cemetery in nearby Bari the next afternoon. Manduria was now down to 35 combat ships and 350 brokenhearted men.

Joe and his crew practiced formation flying and bomb aiming as best they could with a replacement instructor. They needed to keep their skills sharp, but more, they needed to forget what had happened. They had not flown much since leaving the United States and it felt good to be back as a team, despite everything. Joe was now making $96.00 a month. With a 50 per cent bonus for flying time, he was pulling in $144.00, enough to send a few dollars home to his mother at the end of every month.

Joe was elated when the day came to leave the mud hole of Manduria behind. Early in the afternoon of January 17, new orders were cut. The entire squadron was ordered closer to the front. It was none too soon for Joe.

His destination was Fortunato Cesare Airdrome in Lecce, a short 30 minute flight away. From this former enemy fighter base near Galentina, in the middle of wine and olive country on the Italian heel, the 415th Squadron of the 98th Bomb Group made final preparations for battle. Joe was about to join the next generation of fighting men from the Maloney family.

CHAPTER THREE

An Uneasy Peace

There never was a good war, or a bad peace.
Benjamin Franklin
September 11, 1783

When the Treaty of Versailles was signed in Paris in 1919, bringing to an end four-and-a-half years of apocalyptic sacrifices in the Great War, a new kind of struggle began to emerge. Not since the Napoleonic Wars, a hundred years earlier, had Europe been dealt such a severe blow. Former enemies, crippled by gigantic war debts and a scale of mass destruction and social upheaval the world had never seen, faced a bleak future. But such was not the case across the ocean, where America's wartime industry soon turned its vast potential to peacetime production. The land of plenty was just waking up from a long nightmare.

Motor cars, bathtubs, electric refrigerators and radios quickly became the new touchstones of progress. With the new decade came a new way of life. The business of America was, indeed, business, the triumph of a great industrial development that began in the days of the Civil War. By the early 1920's, the United States was in full stride. After all, the "war to end all wars" was finally over. It was time to get on with living.

That's exactly what Joseph Maloney and Rose Bouchet decided to do. Rose, in particular, was anxious to leave behind her weary past. Her early childhood in Norfolk, Connecticut, had been filled with stories of how her father had been forced to leave his home country when just a young lad. The end of the Franco-Prussian War in 1871 left France aggrieved by the loss of Alsace-Lorraine. Fifteen years later, Paul Bouchet was facing a life of compulsory military service in his troubled homeland. At the tender age of 16, he figured he would be better off taking his chances in America and decided to go with his instincts.

Rose was also trying to cope with a more recent family tragedy. Her brother had been killed in the Great War and she missed him dearly. Paul C. Bouchet died as a result of a gas attack in the Chemin-des-Dames sector of France. Her only other brother, John, had been severely wounded in the same battle. The Bouchet brothers had the dubious distinction of being among the very first casualties of the 26th Division of the New England National Guard. Rose had had her fill of war and talk of war. She needed a breath of fresh air. She knew she had found it in her Joe.

Meanwhile, although growing up was much less traumatic for Joseph Maloney, life was no less intriguing. As a young man, he was particularly proud of the fact that his father had become a U.S. citizen around the turn of the century. Joseph Sr. had emigrated from a small village in the midlands of Ireland near Athlone, on the River Shannon, a place called Castletown-Geoghgan, County West Meath.

In 1885, Joseph Sr. left Ireland to join his two other brothers in Winsted, Connecticut, just down the road from Norfolk. He soon married and had a son. Small and friendly, the two New England towns were nestled away in a pristine corner of this bucolic state. The Maloney's and Bouchet's were practically neighbors. It didn't take long for young Joseph and Rose to meet. After dating only a few times, they, like many other couples after the war, quickly decided to get married. The wedding took place on May 15, 1922. Looking forward to a bright new future in post-war America, the

Left to right: Rose Bouchet (Joe's mother) and Minnie Bouchet (Joe's grandmother). Norfolk, CT, the homestead where Joe was raised by his grandparents after his parents separated, 1925.

newlyweds decided to settle down in Winsted where Joseph drove a delivery truck.

Three cents brought home the April 5, 1923 edition of the *Winsted Evening Citizen.* Crammed among the local news stories on the back page that day was a short notice. "A son was born at the hospital to Mr. and Mrs. Joseph Maloney of Main Street." The baby, born the day before at Winsted Memorial, was given his father's name, Joseph Leo Maloney.

As luck would have it, young Joe would soon be denied a normal family life. When he was only two, his parents separated and he was shipped off to live with his grandparents, Paul and Minnie

Joseph L. Maloney, first Holy Communion, 1930 - 7 years old.

Bouchet, in nearby Norfolk. His mother moved away to another part of the state. He never saw his father again.

Joe got along well with his surrogate parents though, always willing to lend a hand with the chores. He especially liked to work with his grandfather, a stone mason, one of the best in the state. By the time he was a teenager, another important person had entered Joe's life, a man by the name of Lester Roberts. Understanding the importance of two wheel transportation – Lester had been a motorcycle dispatcher with the 26th Division of the New England National Guard in the Great War – he presented Joe with a brand new bicycle on his 13th birthday.

Lester Roberts had been in a nearby trench waiting for orders on the day his brother, Joseph, along with Paul Bouchet were fatally attacked at Chemin-des-Dames on March 17, 1918. A few days before Lester gave Joe his brand new bike, he had married Rose Maloney. Joe now laid claim to two uncles who had been killed in the war. His young life was already full of twists and turns.

Joe grew very fond of his stepfather. Although he lived with his grandparents, he spent a lot of time with Lester, especially when it came time to go hunting in the kaleidoscope of a Connecticut autumn. It was Lester Roberts, the seasoned campaigner from the Great War, who instilled in Joe a keen respect for the power of a gun, and how it just might save his life one day.

As time went by Joe grew closer to his mother, rekindling a bond that was never really broken. And, although he never did see his father alive again, he did get to say good-bye to him at his funeral. Joseph Maloney died in Baltimore in 1935 of spinal meningitis. He was only 35. By the Spring of 1938, young Joe was polishing off his sophomore year at Gilbert High and looking forward to a brighter future.

Always too busy to take any notice of the political rumblings in some far off place like Europe, Joe was blissfully unaware that Germany was poised to annex Austria and the Sudentenland, and that the insipid British policy of appeasement was about to collapse like a house of cards. Yet, like most Americans, still wrapped up in post-World War I isolation and still immersed in the torment of the Great Depression, Joe would have been surprised to learn that Germany had built up quite a sizable nest egg of military might. On September 1, 1939, Hitler launched his plan for a grand Fatherland with a massive air and ground assault against Poland.

For Joe Maloney and many of his friends, the first casualty of war was their education. They quit school the minute they heard about the outbreak. It just seemed to be the right thing to do at the time, as Joe later recalls. Although the United States remained neutral, Joe never wavered in his conviction that he would be dragged into the fight one day. He remembered his grandfather's words during the Depression that the scrap metal the United States had been shipping to Japan would someday come back.

Quickly losing interest in his future, Joe's attention turned to fast cars and quick money. He landed a job at the Gilbert Clock Company in Winsted, working up to the position of nightshift supervisor. A five day, 60-hour week brought home $14, good enough for a down-payment on a second hand Ford Coupe. Best of all, it had a radio. That's how he heard all about the London Blitz and Churchill's many stirring "We Shall Fight" speeches. The more he heard, the more he realized the United States would not be spared from the fight for much longer.

As he saw more and more of

Joseph L. Maloney - 19 years old, Hartford, CT., 1942, the year before he joined the U.S.A.A.F.

his future slipping away, Joe decided there was only one thing left to do, buy a new car and raise a little hell. But that would take more money than he was making at the old clock factory. He soon talked his way into a higher paying job at the experimental department of Pratt and Whitney Aircraft Corporation in nearby East Hartford. He ran lathes, milling machines and drill presses that turned out prototype engine parts. It was exacting work but he figured he could use the discipline. It also gave him the cash he needed to buy his dream car.

On the morning of December 7, 1941, Japan attacked the American naval base at Pearl Harbor. Over 100 carrier based Japanese fighters and bombers sank or badly damaged eight battleships and 10 other naval vessels at anchor or in dry-dock and 188 U.S. planes were destroyed on the ground. Nearly 3,000 military personnel were dead or dying.

As usual, Joe heard all about it on his car radio. But not even his brand new Buick Sports Coupe could take the sting out of the news that particular day. The United States had been stabbed in the back, and, of course, that meant war. America's scrap metal had indeed come back from Japan, just as Joe's grandfather always said it would. Joe's long journey to his new home in Lecce, Italy had already begun.

CHAPTER FOUR

Into the Heart of Darkness

Farewell happy fields
where joy forever dwells:
Hail horrors, hail!

Paradise Lost
John Milton (1667)

Squinting against the bright sun rising slowly in the eastern sky one spring day in 1917, a junior British military clerk was mystified by what he saw. Craning his neck for a better view from his second floor office window in downtown London, the young man saw what looked like "a shoal of little silver fish darting about, miles up in the sky." He didn't know what to make of it. What was really up there, although he had no way of knowing, was a diamond formation of twin-engine German Gotha bombers. The clerk along with a lot of other Londoners were about to experience something completely new in warfare.

With only limited range and modest speed, the 14 Gothas, nevertheless, delivered a deadly payload that fateful day; 162 people were killed, including 46 children slaughtered while still sitting at their desks at school. Another 432 Londoners were injured. Nobody thought to take cover. They had little reason to. London had never before been bombed during broad daylight. It was a wake up call the world would never forget.

The concept of strategic bombing had thus been born, although, for the duration of the great war, the bomber remained a limited weapon, crude in performance and employed in a desultory manner. Not until the Spanish Civil War in 1937, when Adolf Hitler demonstrated beyond all doubt the deadly potential of strategic bombing, did the rest of the world begin to sit up and take notice. By the beginning of World War II, the stage was set for the pivotal role to be played by the bomber.

By the time the United States entered the fray, its Army Air Force had little if anything to brag about. It had 3300 combat-ready aircraft to the Navy's 3000 airplanes. Trouble was, they were mostly all obsolete. There was not one heavy four engine bomber to be found anywhere. However, American technology-not to mention the fact that it takes a good enemy to make a good airplane-soon filled the gap.

By early 1944, the USAAF packed a lot more punch than "the shoal of little silver fish" over London 27 years earlier. Aerial bombardment, particularly high altitude precision bombing, had come a long way by the time Joe and his crew opened for business at Fortunato Cesare Airdrome in Lecce.

Joe and his crew immediately went into high gear in preparation for combat. It meant long days of formation flying and bomb aiming. But, realizing everything they did from here on could make the difference between survival or death, they pushed themselves to the point of exhaustion. They practiced and practiced from dawn till dusk. While their training schedule was grueling, the men of the 98th were generally happy about their fate on the ground. Writing to his sister, Ed Brady admitted life wasn't so bad at the front after all.

"Every day is a picnic, strictly an outdoor life. We live in tents scattered around the area and ingenuity runs rampant. Floors of packing crates, stoves from oil cans, old bomb cases, wash basins from helmets, cans, gas tanks, personal water heating systems, any old junk you have we can use. It is a rugged life but its our own. You should see us here."

Conditions were not as primitive for the base commanders of course.

Tent City, Lecce, Italy. Enlisted men's living quarters, Feb./March 1944. Note the mud. Home of 415th Squadron, 98th Bombardment Group and the 15th Air Force.

41

Front row, kneeling, left to right: Wm. Bichefield (navigator), Ed Brady (pilot), Clark Fetterman (bombardier), Fred Streicher (copilot) - Fred was pilot on 2 April 1944. Back row, left to right: Wm. Kollar (asst. radio), Clarence Jensen (engineer), Joe Maloney (armorer gunner), Waldo Akers (gunner), John Reilly (radio man), Art Fleming (ball turret gunner).

Housed in large three-story stone barracks, they had to make do with running water, tile floors and even built-in closets. Only on Fridays and Sundays were their hot showers off limits. But, whether living in a tent or in barracks it made no difference when it came to the elbow grease needed to bring the base up to snuff. Everybody was expected to pitch in.

"In many cases we were repairing our own damage," writes Brady. "The outfit I am with now was bombing these same people and they know it. Still, most of the civilians are glad we are here. They are treated far better by us than by the Germans and also by the Fascist Party. I have been in houses, slept in the same bed and eaten from the same dishes as used by the Germans."

Although the airdrome at Lecce technically came under Italian command, since Italy was now one of the Allies, it was the Americans with their massive presence of heavy bombers who clearly ran the show. The Italians who worked there, many of whom were civilians, played only a supporting role. Everything they did was centered around making the American airmen better warriors. Before long, Ed Brady had a well trained crew on his hands, equaled only by one of the best ships in the USAAF fleet at the time-a B-24 Liberator.

Designed and built by Consolidated Aircraft Company (also built later by Ford and Douglas, and North American), the Liberator was the most advanced strategic bomber in the USAAF next to the Boeing B-17, the already famous Flying Fortress. The pilots loved the Lib. Crews on both bombers were the same size but the B-24s were slightly "hotter," that is they landed a little faster and were slightly more difficult to handle. The Liberator was also bigger. It had a longer range and was also faster than the Fortress. Although designed and built in the United States, it was Great Britain, the first among the Allies to lead them into action, that gave the Liberator its name.

"I wouldn't say the Liberator was much to look at on the ground," Joe admits. "A combat loaded B-24 was so tail-heavy that when the engines were turned off, it slunk down on its tail, there to stay."

Roundish and ungainly in appearance, the four engine, high wing bomber with its tall twin-rudders, inevitably earned some boorish nicknames, *Pregnant Cow, Flying Coffin* and *Flying Boxcar*, among them. B-17 crews referred to them as the "crate the Flying Fortress came in." The strong rivalry between B-17 and B-24 crews was legendary.

But, in the air, the burly B-24 was a picture of grace and style. Originally designed for the more mundane duties of aerial transport, naval reconnaissance and anti-submarine patrols, the *"Flying Boxcar"* proved to be a versatile aircraft. It was also prodigious. Over 18,000 of them were

Maggie's Drawers, 1944.

built, more than any other single aircraft during the entire war. Once in the theatre, each ship was given a crew's individual stamp of approval with a suitable name along with a provocative lady painted on her nose.

"*Maggie's Drawers* already had her name when I first saw her," says Joe of his ship.

According to ground crew chief, Reinie Schweitzer, *Maggie* first joined Joe's 415th Squadron in the mud hole of Manduria, in October of 1943. Joe never knew who *Maggie* was, nor what was so special about her drawers. It was a popular name though. There were three others, a B-24 and two B-17s, by the same name. Joe was proud to be counted among the many lucky men who could brag about getting into *Maggie's Drawers*. Typical of the way he always did things, Ed Brady had won his ship in a coin flip.

"The crew and I were really lucky," he wrote home in 1944. "Bob Fischer and I got here the same time. They had two extra planes. We tossed a coin and I won first choice of a nice new "J" (model) with all turrets and only 160 hours on her and a battle-scarred "D" with two turrets. You can guess which one I took."

Maggie's Drawers came with much improved firepower over the older models. She had new nose and ball turrets along with double bomb bay doors, a complete radio system, navigational equipment and automatic pilot.

Maggie also sported superchargers in her engines, something that would give her extra speed in a pinch, one of the first B-24s to be so equipped. The bomber with serial number 42-73077 and delivered to the USAAF at a cost of $241,924 was one fine ship and Joe thanked his lucky stars for such a lucky break.

Ready as they would ever be, all Joe and his crewmates could do now was wait for their first mission to be posted. Everyday they watched and waited as other airmen went out and sometimes didn't come back. B-24s returned from time-to-time all shot up and worse, with their dead and dying aboard. One afternoon stood out from all the rest as one of their wounded birds tried to get back home.

It happened when Ed Brady and Fred Streicher were pulling control tower duty. Tagging along to keep them company, Joe suddenly heard the unmistakable voice of a combat pilot coming from the two-way radio. "I got severely wounded on board and I have to land," the edgy yet controlled voice pleaded with ground control. "We're out of morphine and my men are screaming with pain."

Joe bolted out of his chair and ran to the window for a better look, trying hard not to think about the terrible nightmare that must have been unfolding inside the bomber. He could see the Liberator zigzagging in the haze beyond the end of the runway. It was all shot up. Yet Brady ordered the pilot to wave off and come in behind the rest of the formation. As cruel and unusual as this sounded, there was always the fear that a crippled ship would crash, tying up the runway and stranding the rest of the fleet. Brady had no choice. It had to be by the book.

"I'm not waiting," came the very agitated reply. "I'm coming in, clearance or not."

Joe was mortified as the stricken plane hove into full view. He could see the ball turret dangling beneath the damaged fuselage. Every pilot knows you can't land a Liberator like that. At least that's what the experts who designed and built the B-24 always said. The few pilots who forgot paid for their mistake with their lives. The Liberator could be very unforgiving if mistreated.

As Joe stared in disbelief, the B-24 slammed hard onto the runway for a perfect three point landing. Actually, it was more like a four point touchdown. The main landing gear and the nose wheel made contact with the hardtop at the same time as the turret, leaving behind a long roostertail of sparks. The bomber screeched to a grinding halt at the end of the runway. Joe shook his head in quiet admiration for a man who had just risked his own command for the sake of his crew. He was also tickled pink that even the experts could be wrong when it came to understanding just how much punishment the B-24 could or could not take.

Early February 1944 ushered in something new for the 98th Bombardment Group, a decided turn in the weather. Rain and heavy fog held an iron grip on any early hopes of striking quickly at the enemy from Lecce. Their missions up until now were spotty at best, with many of the new crews including Joe's yet to see any action. For them, time was the enemy. There was nothing they could do but wait. It wore on their nerves because they lived by a very simple philosophy of survival. The sooner into the fray, the sooner back home. Fifty missions meant stateside for the few airmen lucky enough to survive that long.

Initially, tour completion policy was based on the calculation that an airman had an exposure of four percent non-completion per mission. Therefore at the end of 25 sorties, the casualty exposure equaled 100 percent, and the crew member could be eligible for rotation back to the States. But this was early in the game. As the war progressed and more and more crews were lost, this number was gradually revised upward until, near war's end, 50 missions were required.

The men of the 15th Air Force didn't like this rule change in the middle of the game one bit, but it did offer them at least a glimmer of hope. Unlike ground troops, they at least had something to shoot for. Joe knew some men who had actually reached that magic number, and he hoped that, somehow, their luck would now come to him.

As each day passed, more and more targets of the 98th were no shows. No sooner was a mission posted when it was scrubbed. The airdrome at

Pian del Largo, Italy and a submarine pen at Toulon Harbour, France were spared because of bad weather. Sometimes missions were launched, only to be quickly aborted because the lead plane got lost in the fog or low clouds.

Torrential rain and constant fog became the constant nemesis of the 98th. The airdrome often looked more like a huge lake with the B-24s taking the place of islands. If Manduria were bad, Lecce was worse. Nine missions were canceled in the first 11 days of February alone. This was turning out to be one hell of a place from which to fight a war. Instead of dwelling on the odds of getting through 50 missions, Joe started to wonder if he would ever even get one under his belt.

The official logs of the 98th Bombardment Group reflected the depth of frustration felt by everyone, air and ground crews alike. February 11, 1944 was typical.

"Today we got as far as warming up the engines. To break the monotony of silence a new siren blasted away, scaring the daylights out of the Italian workers. Remembering the time the 98th plastered this airdrome, they are taking no chances. The men on the line are sure catching heck these days. Bomb loads are changed as much as four times a day."

Finally, late in the evening of February 16, the weather broke. The 98th was issued new marching orders. On the operations bulletin board were the names of 34 pilots on the next day's roster. Ed Brady's was among them. Joe was about to experience his first epochal mission.

The posting of any mission set off a familiar pattern on the base at Lecce. The handling of fear was a big part of any assignment for veteran and green crews alike. Activity, especially among those who were on notice for the next morning, became sharply focused. A few of them had a quiet drink with their friends.

The airmen who chose to linger in front of the bulletin board speculated about the likely target. Others quietly shuffled off to the privacy of their tents to wrap themselves in warm thoughts of home. They wrote letters to their loved ones, as if this might be their last chance. In some cases it was. A few poured over their dog-eared letters from wives and girlfriends. Their tenuous connection with home offered a momentary respite from the punishing hours of pre-mission stress.

"There was no real doomsday atmosphere," one of Joe's buddies observed. "Just that those flying sought the company of close friends or, at the other extreme, went solitary in their own thoughts. There would be a few jokes, but not many. Nobody in their right mind would ever try to enter into the conversations if he was not aircrew, with the possible exception of some ground crew chiefs, who had formed a special rapport with the crew who flew the airplanes they serviced."

Joe wasn't exactly overwhelmed when he found out about his first mission. He knew it had to come sometime and he figured now was as good a time as any. After all, this is what he had been trained for. He accepted his fate with the realization that there was a job to be done. It was that simple. Life came down to the basics now, with survival the only game in town. Nothing else mattered. Absolutely nothing.

The more seasoned airmen around him would have agreed with this stoic point of view. Bomber crews were fatalists on the whole; you bought it or you didn't. Either way, they wasted little energy in worrying about their future. Besides, everyone was convinced that it would be the "other guy" and not him when it came time to buy the farm.

At 4:00 a.m., February 17, an unsettling night of fitful sleep came to an abrupt end with the unwelcomed appearance of the squadron's duty officer at Joe's tent flaps. It was an ungodly hour, but cursing and swearing made no difference. Preflight preparations always began at this time, give or take an hour or so. It was just one more thing the airmen couldn't change. It was time to face the music and that was that.

Ed Brady was already up. It was one of the perks of command that he would have gladly given up. But no such luck. The captain always had to be the first one on deck whenever his crew was on call. Brady then woke up Fred Streicher, who in turn roused the other officers. The rest of the enlisted men got the word from the flight engineer. None of them really needed any wakeup call that first morning. Sleep would not come, no matter how hard they tried to put aside their fears and anxieties.

Exchanging silent glances, the men splashed cold water on their faces from their inverted steel helmets, each lost in the privacy of his own world. Afraid of betraying any signs of fear, Joe and his crew mates instinctively avoided direct eye contact as they hauled on their outer clothing, picked up their gear and trudged off to the mess tent for powdered eggs, dried toast, bacon and coffee. It would be a day to tell their children about, if they lived long enough to have any.

Although there were separate eating arrangements for the officers and the enlisted men, crews usually ate together before a mission. Rank was rarely pulled in the tight unit of a combat crew, especially at such a critical time. Joe appreciated this small luxury, as he picked at his food and swallowed what little he could. He took it easy on the black coffee not wanting to overload his kidneys on the bumpy ride ahead.

A small fleet of trucks then shuttled the men from the mess compound to Group Headquarters for the mission briefing. Usually everyone attended, but, in Joe's case, only the officers went. He and the other enlisted men wanted to be with their ship as soon as possible to make sure everything was ready.

In typical military fashion, the pre-dawn briefing was short and to the point. There wasn't a moment to lose. At the appointed hour, the group commander strode into the briefing hut while everyone stood to attention. The commander called "seats" while another officer unveiled a map with a red ribbon pointing the way to the target. This was always the moment of truth. Depending on whether the crews considered the mission a milk run or not, either a gasp of dismay or a collective sigh of relief filled the room.

The briefing officers then outlined in detail the known flak positions and possible enemy fighters to expect along the mission route. They gave the IP (Initial Point), from which the formation turned onto the bomb run, length of the bomb run, and direction of the rally away from the target. The bomber crews were also given the number of friendly fighters they could expect for penetration, target and withdrawal cover.

Their target on the morning of February 17 would be Genzeno, a German beachhead near Anzio, in Nazi occupied west-central Italy. The briefing officers predicted heavy flak and possible enemy fighters. As each pulled in a deep breath, Brady and Streicher knew this would not be a cakewalk-more like baptism by fire.

A separate board to one side of the briefing room displayed the group formation with aircraft numbers and pilots names listed. Brady was given a "flimsy," or fragmentary battle order, which depicted the formation and the mission codes for that day. This "bible" always accompanied every pilot on board his aircraft.

The flight officers were also brought up to date on the latest security arrangements. Color codes for flares that signaled important orders, like precise take-off time for the group leader, were changed every half hour. Brady and Streicher were reminded that there would be radio silence once they were airborne and that no radio instructions from the ground were to be followed except for mission recall. Before the briefing broke up, a weather officer gave a forecast, and finally, when all else was done, the chaplain offered a prayer.

Clark Fetterman and William Birchfield, along with the other bombardiers and navigators, went on to detailed technical briefings, while radio operator John Reilly was briefed again, to make sure he had all the right codes. After that, the officers were driven to the flight line. By the time they arrived, flight engineer Clarence Jensen and the gunners were already ·aboard *Maggie's Drawers* helping the ground crew top off the gas tanks with 2,700 gallons of pure one-hundred octane. Joe was busy elsewhere in the ship. As armorer-gunner, he was responsible for all in-flight weaponry, including the four power turrets, the two flexible waist guns and, of course, the bomb stations. If anything jammed or malfunctioned during the mission, it would be his duty to fix it.

Brady and Streicher climbed into the cockpit to stow their parachutes, Mae Wests, oxygen masks and other personal equipment behind their seats. Climbing back down, they did their walkabout inspection under the steely-gray shimmer of the breaking dawn. As usual, Streicher was drawing hard on a cigarette as he kicked each tire.

Joe had hardly noticed the awakening sky from deep inside the cavernous Liberator. He was too busy checking and rechecking each bomb, making sure their shackles, which held them on the racks, were placed properly, and that all the arming wires were correctly installed. He didn't want any foul ups, especially on his first outing. Most of all he didn't want to have to be the one to shuffle across the catwalk in the cold rarefied air of 25,000 feet, all because of something he had neglected to do before the flight. Keeping busy also helped him avoid thinking too much about the mission.

Joe inspected the bomb fuses to make sure the cotter pins were in place in case of an extra bumpy ride. After all, when fully loaded, he knew his plane was nothing more than a flying bomb. It could get pretty rough in the path of a flak burst. He also tested the power turrets with their double 50-caliber machine guns for azimuth and elevation. And one more thing. He made sure the machine gun belts were full and that there were plenty of extra cases of bullets. Bombardier Clark Fetterman double-checked his top secret Norden Bombsight for accuracy. With navigation and communications finally checked out, *Maggie's Drawers* was ready to go.

With the pre-flight inspections completed, there was just enough time for each airman to look after some last minute personal needs, like a run to the latrine. Although the B-24s had "pee" tubes, sit-down bowel movements were definitely not recommended during combat. A green flair from a Very pistol at headquarters signaled engine start-up and roll-out to take-off position. This was it. The mission was a go.

Joe glanced down at his wristwatch. It was shortly before 8:30, four and a half hours since reveille. It felt more like a lifetime. It was time to go. Hot roaring exhaust suddenly exploded into the cold still air from 36 tightly-coiled heavy bombers on the tarmac at Lecce. Each pilot had to wait his turn to see which airplane he was to follow onto the runway in order to quickly establish the proper combat formation once airborne. There was absolute demand for order and sequence if the whole thing had any chance of working. Otherwise, there would be nothing but a mad traffic jam. This is where a pilot's skill and training really came in handy.

The "flimsy" told Brady when and where to squeeze *Maggie's Drawers* into the prearranged take-off slot. Joe checked his watch again. 8:32 a.m. He noticed a slight tremble in his hands. The lead plane was poised for the clear-to-roll signal from ground control. The rest of the fleet could do nothing more than follow the leader. If the lead made a mistake, or somehow the mission didn't go as planned, every crewman who followed knew it would be Judas leading the lambs to slaughter.

The squadron commander raised his arm and brought it down in a forward motion along the flight line. The lead pilots acknowledged the signal for take-off. At precisely 8:45 a.m., the Liberators began to roll down the runway. As *Maggie's Drawers* lurched forward, Joe began to realize just how much life had changed in the short 12 months and 12 days since he had taken that early morning bus ride out of Norfolk, Connecticut to join the army. He figured life would never be quite the same after this. He figured right.

Ed Brady had already pushed the throttles to about 30 inches of manifold pressure until he could feel the airplane vibrate. When Fred Streicher popped the brakes, *Maggie's Drawers* lunged forward and waddled down the runway, its four-14 cylinder engines straining every inch of the way under the tremendous load. At 120 miles per hour, Brady pulled back on the stick and the sluggish bomber nudged skyward. He figured he would be at his optimum climbing speed within a matter of minutes. He figured wrong.

"We were overloaded with bombs," Joe remembers. "We went up to about 100 feet but couldn't get any higher."

The labored B-24 narrowly skimmed over the tree tops for 15 long, nail-biting minutes. Where were those fancy new superchargers when they really needed them, Joe wondered? Finally, after much coaxing from the pilots, and a lot of cursing and swearing from the rest of the crew, *Maggie's Drawers* slowly picked up speed and began to climb. But, by then, they were way out of formation. With no radio communications, all they could do now was a quick search to try to find the rest of the fleet.

Instead of inviting complete disaster, the always resourceful Texan pilot poured on the coal, caught up with the other B-24s within a matter of minutes, and deftly slipped his ship into his designated rendezvous point to complete the formation. Luck was finally with them. They had made it. At least this far. *Maggie's Drawers* took up the aft position in one of several seven plane boxes-a standard combat formation for the 15th AAF - as the B-24s surged towards the beachhead target, now only a short flight away.

The box design, within each staggered combat formation, allowed the gunners to shoot at enemy fighters without hitting each other. It also offered each individual bomber the benefit of the group's collective defensive firepower. But, there was one hitch. Not all of the positions within each box were equally protected. Crews going out on their first few missions inevitably found themselves relegated to the most vulnerable slot of all, at the tail end. If they paid their dues and survived, only then did they earn the right to move forward in the box to a more secure position, if and when one became available. When that happened, there were always mixed emotions since it usually came at the expense of losing a buddy.

Joe was rightfully concerned about his own hapless position that morning since he knew that 90% of enemy air attacks always came from the rear. As usual, there wasn't a thing he could do about it either. Sitting with his knees up against his chest and his shoulders wedged between his twin 50s, Joe thought long and hard about the enemy radio broadcasts he often listened to back at the base.

Axis Sally, the German version of the more famous Tokyo Rose, always had the nasty habit of telling the American airmen exactly where each day's mission was going on the morning they were leaving. This morning was no different. It was Hitler's little way of thumbing his nose at the Allies. German intelligence took a back seat to nobody. Right now that really bugged the hell out of Joe.

CHAPTER FIVE

Gladiators of the Air

Theirs not to make reply,
Theirs not to reason why,
Theirs but to do or die.

> *The Charge of the Light Brigade*
> *Alfred, Lord Tennyson (1854)*

The flight of the Liberators to the beachhead target was soon fraught with trouble. Nine of the B-24s were forced to turn back. A few experienced jammed turrets; some had engine trouble; while one bomber simply got lost. Headquarters always assumed, and assumed correctly, that part of every formation would never reach the target. So it came as no surprise to Joe when the remaining 25 ships received no orders to return to base. Nothing was allowed to get in the way of a mission, not even something as minor as a few missing airplanes.

As the group leader turned at the Initial Point that would take the rest of the formation on its predetermined heading over the bomb alley, Joe remained vigilant at his post. Trained as a tail gunner, he was, nevertheless, assigned the waist window on his first outing. The more critical tail gun was left to the more experienced hands of a veteran airman seconded from another crew. The switch had been made at the last minute. Joe didn't mind one little bit. Actually, he felt relieved. Living seemed to be a higher priority than a bruised ego at that moment.

Clutching the handles of his flexible 50 calibre machine gun, Joe began to wonder when something might happen. He didn't have long to wait as day suddenly turned into night. The Germans called it Flugzeugabwehrkannonen. The Allies knew it as flak. By either name, it was just as deadly.

From the color of the flak bursts, Ed Brady knew the Germans were firing their range finding rounds. But, after a few more seconds, when the orange blossoms turned to black smoke with flaming red centers, he knew the enemy had figured out the correct fuse altitude settings on their big 88 guns below. Depending on how much punch the Germans packed in each shell, the flak could be almost any color: white, black, mustard, red and even lavender. But common to all flak was the jagged steel fragments that were blown out in all directions for hundreds of feet. Brady noticed the bursts were pitch black this time, not a good sign. By 1944, the Germans had their air raid defenses down to a science. Their high velocity, fast firing anti-aircraft guns could punch through a high flying formation of bombers without mercy.

The 88s were also radar directed and often mounted on railway tracks for quick relocation. The shells, fused to explode at the height at which the bombers were flying, could take a terrible toll. It was the bane of every Allied intelligence officer at briefing time and Joe now knew why. He could hear the unmistakable "wuff, wuff, wuff" of the shell blasts under his wings and the sprinkles of shrapnel slamming against the ship like shovelfuls of gravel as *Maggie's Drawers* plowed through the onslaught. There was little a heavy bomber could do about flak. Evasive action was out of the question. That would only break up the air armada, and, if that happened, all hell would break loose because everybody depended on everybody else to complete their perilous journey. Mutual protection would be sacrificed and, worse, the mission lost. It had to be "steady as she goes" for every ship in the formation, no matter what. The Germans were just as determined not to let this happen.

In the nose of *Maggie's Drawers,* bombardier Clark Fetterman was poised to toggle his payload, watching carefully for the signal from the lead ship. The success or failure of the mission would now depend on the skills of the lead bombardier who worked the crosshairs of his Norden bombsight to adjust course. The bombardier, not the pilot, was flying the plane at this point. He had to compensate for rate, the speed the ship was approaching the target, and drift, the strength and direction of the cross-winds. Crosswinds were especially unpredictable in the middle of a flak barrage. A single deputy lead plane was their only backup insurance.

All of the other crews were ready to drop their payloads on the first bombs out of either the lead or deputy lead planes. The Liberators were now at their most vulnerable point for they had no choice but to fly straight and level in order to release their bombs properly. They were sitting ducks and they knew it. So did the Germans. Hitting a target from five miles up demanded calm and precision, despite the incredible pounding the bombers were taking from the flak. But, they had a job to do and they were going to deliver. "Bombs away," Fetterman called out at last on the intercom, as the olive drab explosives trained out of the ship's belly right on cue. Brady didn't need to be told. He had already felt the ship lurch in his controls. Along with her spent fuel, *Maggie's Drawers* was suddenly 15,000 pounds lighter than her near fatal takeoff weight.

The flak was still heavy as the Liberators rallied away from the target. Their exit route was a predetermined 170 mile per hour slithering descent. Some of the pilots wanted to go faster, but the group had to protect the slower crippled ships. Joe noticed that one of the other bombers had a prop feathered and was leaving behind a greasy black smoke trail. At its best possible speed, the formation beat it for home.

Within minutes, *Maggie's Drawers* fell silent, save for the comforting whir of her smooth Pratt and Whitney engines. They had made it out of the flak field alive! Joe took off his steel helmet but kept a sullen watch over the fragile calm. He found it odd that he was sweating in the freezing cold.

Suddenly, Streicher's voice burst through the ship's intercom warning everybody to be on the alert. That could only mean one thing.

"Flak dead ahead," the co-pilot thundered the next minute.

As more deadly rounds of explosives whumped against the sides of the fuselage, Joe clutched his head with both hands. He was in trouble.

"I'm hit, I'm hit!" he blurted into his throat mike, as waist gunner Waldo Akers jumped in to see what all the fuss was about.

"How bad?" came the anxious reply from the cockpit.

"Don't know, but I'm hit," Joe called back in rising panic.

A relentless high-pitch screech rippled through Joe's headphones as he frantically groped for telltale signs of blood. He yanked off his steel helmet for a closer inspection. The noise stopped. Then it suddenly hit him.

"My earphones must have shorted out when I put my helmet back on in such a hurry," he recalls sheepishly. "The noise howling in my ears made me feel like I had been hit."

Once he realized what had happened, Joe gave the thumbs-up sign but it was too late to save face. Akers was already laughing hysterically. Joe would never live this one down. It was a long flight home.

While the bone weary crews tried to unwind back at the base, their B-24s were inspected, repaired, refueled, and restocked with bombs for the next time. *Maggie's Drawers* had sustained only a few pot marks for her troubles.

Mission 187 for the 98th went down in the books as an operational success and 6.8 hours of combat time were chalked up along with 16,500

1944 flight with 465th Bomb Group B-24 in formation.

pounds of bombs dropped. Not a bad day's work. An airman from one of the other ships had been severely wounded by flak and two Purple Hearts were issued. But, all 25 Liberators managed to get back home in one piece. Everything considered, Joe had had a good day. However, his euphoria was short lived.

Five days later, twenty B-24s left Lecce to join a larger formation from other allied bases to bomb the Messerschmitt factory in Regensburg, Germany. *Maggie's Drawers* stood down as over a hundred other heavies hit the target. The Germans responded with deadly force and, this time, the bombers were mauled. Fourteen ships were lost, including one named *Black Magic*.

Aboard that doomed B-24 was Ed Brady. New airmen were routinely split up and temporarily assigned to more experienced crews for battle conditioning. On February 22, it had been Brady's turn to take a few lessons from veteran combat pilot Don Mallas. As it turned out, the two of them had a lot in common. Mallas was the first pilot to ever take *Maggie's Drawers* into battle. After hearing about the fate of *Black Magic*, Joe wondered bitterly about the odds of Brady and Mallas getting shot down together in a completely different airplane.

It was bright and sunny when the decimated remnants of the 98th staggered home to Lecce at the end of that terrible day. The weather did little to lighten the mood. Joe's crew was grounded until further notice. They had lost an excellent pilot and a dear friend. Joe would miss his wrestling buddy. Back in Casablanca the two of them used to spend hours throwing each other around on the hot sand just to kill the boredom. They never let the difference in their ranks get in the way of a good friendship.

By now, the score card for the air war over Europe gave passing marks to both sides. German flak and fighters continued to take a heavy toll of Allied bombers as Joe and his crew were painfully aware. On the other hand, the bombers, increasingly accompanied by new long-range fighters, were beginning to reap a heavy harvest of enemy fighters. Although German aircraft production was not immediately affected by the constant hail of bombs, the Luftwaffe was losing more and more of its well trained and experienced fighter pilots. The 98th found itself caught in the midst of a nasty war of attrition.

Germany, correctly believing that the American effort would only grow, brought in more and more day fighters from the Eastern Front and the Mediterranean to defend the Fatherland. American losses soon mounted to a staggering 18.2 percent of missions deployed. Intense cold, deafening noise, and, now, only a one in three chance of completing a tour of duty, were among the pitiful prospects facing the bomber crews. By early 1944, B-17s and B-24s were dropping like flies. With unbounded grit, nevertheless, the USAAF plodded on.

The assumption that the Flying Fortresses, and later the Liberators, could defend themselves against enemy fighter attacks was dead wrong. It was based on the misguided belief that these impressive four-engine bombers, flying in staggered groups in tight formations, could muster over a hundred machine gunners to ward off enemy attack. But German fighters, much faster than the lumbering bombers, were often armed with cannons or rockets, which allowed them to attack out of range. Flak damage often allowed enemy fighters to pick off the crippled bombers at will.

To make matters worse for the Americans, the Norden Bombsight, the backbone of high altitude precision bombing, was often rendered useless in the persistent overcast skies of Europe. The top secret weapon was supposed to be able to put a bomb in a pickle barrel from 20,000 feet. Ultimately, the facts did not bear out the claim. Barely one in five bombs ever landed within a 1,000 feet of the aiming point. By the time Ed Brady's crew got into action, the best efforts of the Allies were, simply, not good enough.

Europe's "soft underbelly" was turning out to be a lot more like tough old shoe leather. German factories were humming with activity. Bombing seemed to only spur the enemy to work even harder, just like the Brits had already discovered during the Blitz. The memoirs of Albert Speer, Reichsminster in charge of Nazi war materiel, noted that production actually increased and reached a peak in 1944, three times what it was in 1941, despite the intensive Allied bombing. It was clear that the Luftwaffe had to be dealt a severe blow, or the great invasion of Europe in the spring could never begin. Hitler's Festung Europa (Fortress Europe) would have to be taken by even greater force, despite the daunting Allied losses.

Siege warfare, so familiar in the trenches of the Great War that claimed the lives of so many men like Joseph Roberts and Paul Bouchet, had come full circle in spite of the best efforts of the British and Americans not to repeat this hard lesson of history. It would be a fight to the bitter end, a fight Joe and his crew were anxious to resume. They were still grounded though, relegated to the status of mere spectators, while everyone else around them were gearing up for the big finish.

New attacks to be delivered by the 15th Air Force, including Joe's 98th, were against single engine fighter plants at Wierner Neustadt and Regensburg, which produced 500 out of the enemy's total of 650 Me 109s per month. Ball bearing targets at Steyr, Klosterle and Schweinfurt also lay within reach. What enemy aircraft did make it to the armadas of heavy bombers would be shot down by the new long range escort, the P-51 Mustang, which had just arrived to supplement the short range Lockheed P-38 Lightning and the Republic P-47 Thunderbolt. At least that was the grand Allied plan.

When Ed Brady was shot down, the nine men he left behind had a big void to fill. They knew the army had a habit of replacing missing crewmen with someone from the "outside", meaning they now faced a real possibility of flying into combat with a pilot they hadn't trained with, didn't know and almost certainly couldn't trust. Joe was beside himself and so was the rest of his crew. Facing the unknown was absolutely terrifying.

From stories he had heard, he knew many bomber pilots found it a strain just to cope with the everyday problems of taking off, flying and landing a heavy aircraft in one piece, before even beginning to come to terms with the enemy. Hundreds of B-17s and B-24s were being lost in all

B-24 flightline, Lecce, Italy. Standing down after a mission.

sorts of misadventures, from collisions and bombs falling on friendly air-craft below, to botched takeoffs and landings. In many of the cases he had heard about, the enemy had played no part. Joe and his crewmates wanted a top notch pilot and that was that.

"We pleaded with headquarters," he says, "not to split us up and ship us all over the Mediterranean and England just to top up some other crews."

It was a long, nail biting wait, but, ultimately, the army saw it their way. *Maggie's Drawers* was finally assigned a new pilot. A new pilot with a familiar face. When Fred Streicher moved into the left seat of the cockpit, Joe couldn't have been happier. Finally, there was something to cheer about amidst the mournful offerings of the air war. His crew was back to fight another day. With the loss of Ed Brady still fresh on their minds, they were determined more than ever to deliver a savage rabbit kick to the enemy.

Most successful bomber pilots were often not measured by their brilliant flying. More important was their ability to avoid unnecessary risk and provide leadership and discipline to their crews. Like Brady, Streicher was such a man as far as Joe and the rest of the crew were concerned. Streicher was not the sort of guy to bark out orders. He made requests. He never let rank get in the way of running a good ship. Streicher trusted the judgment of his crewmen and they returned the favor.

That's not to say he ran a slack ship. He didn't. Idle chitchat on the intercom, for instance, was forbidden. *Maggie's Drawers* had a reputation for being a "quiet" ship and it would stay that way under Streicher, even in the heat of battle. No one ever raised hell or goofed off during a mission. If a crewman had nothing pertinent to say about the status of the ship, he would know enough to keep his mouth shut. Staying alert for enemy fighters was a full time job. This was not the case with all crews. Joe knew of one replacement gunner from another outfit who came back horrified after circling the target while the entire crew sang *"Happy Birthday"* on the intercom to their 21-year old pilot.

The army did bring in an "outsider" to fill the co-pilot's seat. George Morrell, a slightly built warrant officer with dirty blonde hair, was the new kid on the block. The lad from Patterson, New Jersey, was all of 20.

March 2, 1944 brought bright blue skies to Lecce and word of another mission. At the pre-dawn briefing, *Maggie's Drawers* was assigned her usual aft position in one of the seven ship boxes. It was now Fred Streicher's turn to experience the grim burden of command. The wait was never easy. Even veteran pilots admitted to that simple but irrefutable truth.

"You were awakened before you'd hardly had any sleep, walk to chow and then take what was to me that horrible truck ride to the briefing room," remembers one of Joe's friends. "Horrible because, as a farm boy, I had seen my father load cattle on a truck to take them to the slaughterhouse. Every time I got in that army truck I felt like I was one of those animals."

Death or imprisonment, if you didn't come back, were the stark choices facing every combat crew before each mission. If an airman failed to contain his fear, he would soon be tied into knots, useless to himself, his crew and, worst of all, to the mission's success. The sheer terror of letting one's buddies down was usually enough for most of them to at least try to suppress the constant fear welling up their throats. It was something Joe and his crewmates had to fight everyday.

The 98th had orders to provide tactical support to Allied ground troops near the Italian city of Anzio. The mission plan called for a short flight up and across the "boot" to the target, which lay just south of Rome.

German ground troops were preventing Allied soldiers from establishing an important beachhead in the area, so the heavies were being called in to deliver the knock-out punch. Twenty-nine Liberators from Lecce formed part of a much larger assault group. It didn't take long for all hell to break loose over the target.

The flak batteries pounded relentlessly as the thin-skinned B-24s droned through the swirls of black smoke and the murderous streams of red-hot metal over Anzio. Scrunched inside his tail turret, Joe felt every tremble, every shutter of his mad journey through the leaden caldron. A deafening explosion near the tail skidded *Maggie's Drawers* sideways for one terrifying moment as a flak blast slammed into the stabilizers.

From his post, far removed from the rest of the crew, it occurred to Joe that he could be dead for quite some time before anybody noticed. He braced himself at his guns when something caught his attention out of the corner of his eye. He quickly glanced to the left. A bomber at 3 o'clock was peeling off from the formation with her left inboard engine ablaze. From the markings on the huge vertical stabilizers, he knew he didn't know the crew personally, thank God.

Bomber crews usually didn't worry as much about the relative ability of their ships to absorb this kind of punishment, as they did about a single piece of flak ripping through the ship and piercing their bodies. Their last line of defense was a flak jacket. Analysis of wounds inflicted on crews early in the war revealed 70% were the result of low velocity fragments, the kind that could be stopped by a protective garment.

The flak jackets that came later were largely successful against 88mm flak shrapnel and 20mm cannon shell fragments from enemy fighters. They reduced air crew injuries by 60 percent. This, however, was of little comfort to Joe. The only way he could shoehorn his bulky frame into the tail turret was by leaving behind his steel and canvas vest. The removable armor plating inside his tiny bubble also had to go. The only things that separated him from the outside world were his flimsy cotton flight suit and two inches of glass. He felt naked.

The flak was still pounding in his ears as Joe felt the deep rumble of the bomb bay doors creak open. Almost instantly the temperature inside the aircraft plunged to -40° Fahrenheit or centigrade, it made no difference. No matter how you measured it, it was still freezing cold at 22,000 feet. To add to the misery, most B-24 pilots didn't dare use their cockpit heaters at this critical phase. Fueled by gasoline, they only added to the fire hazard in case of a flak hit. Joe was grateful for his electrically heated flight suit, but he worried about the flimsy wires.

"If a wire broke, which could easily happen in the panic of combat, you could get frostbite without even knowing it," he says. "I saw guys with gangrene in their fingers by the time their hands thawed out back on the ground."

The tight formation of heavies made pass after pass over the Anzio target, dropping 90,600 pounds of bombs. After four and a half hours of hammering away, the 98th Group broke off and clawed for home. German troop concentrations took a beating that day. Allied ground forces could now advance.

Crawling from his turret as the B-24s began their descent over friendly airspace, Joe noticed a nasty gash on his left leg. As the icy interior of the aircraft began to melt, he felt a sharp pain. That's when he saw blood oozing from a tear in his flight suit just below his knee-cap. He refused to report the wound out of fear of being cut from the crew. It was one of his greatest fears. He knew he was lucky and it was better to keep his mouth shut. The post mission drink of rye whiskey helped put his flesh wound behind him. While the one shot of booze was always a high point whenever a crew came back, the coffee and donuts were another matter entirely.

"The Air Force always gave us the drink for free," he says. "But the Red Cross had the bloody nerve to charge us 15 cents for a coffee and donut whenever we got back."

After putting his life on the line, this was too much. To top it all off, Joe knew his family was already donating money to the Red Cross back home to help in the war effort. Yet, he was expected to dip into his own pocket for such a small reward. He knew the Red Cross did good work, but that was hardly the point. He felt ripped off and, worse, unappreciated. As usual, his grumbling never changed a thing.

After the mission debriefing, it was back to the tedious wait for the next call to duty. Airmen who returned from combat usually made a conscious effort to block out their memories of the previous hours. The instinct not to dwell on the horrendous odds of buying the farm kept them going. So long as they believed there was a next time and a next, they could somehow cope.

As time went by, the men of the 98th found everyday life in Lecce more and more trying. This was a product of more than just their combat experiences. Even though they had all grown up in the mean and lean years of the Great Depression, they just couldn't get used to the unbelievable poverty and terrible squalid conditions that surrounded them. The war had exacted a heavy price on the Italian civilians, first from the Allies, and then from the retreating Germans. Hunger and desperation were everywhere, and nowhere was this more painfully obvious than on the faces of innocent little children.

Joe was greatly bothered by the daily spectacle of seven and eight year olds huddling over the garbage cans next to the base mess. Rain or shine, they were always there, day in and day out, picking through the leftovers to fill their old rusty tin cans. Little food ever left the base as garbage. The airmen felt more and more guilty each time they sat down for a meal, knowing many hungry little eyes were staring back at them. Although army policy forbade the feeding of civilians, Joe and the others always made sure there was something left over on their trays when they pushed away from the table. A couple of weeks before he was shot down, Ed Brady wrote home to tell about the desperate plight of the Italians.

"The people at home can never realize what it is like here until they have seen it," he observed on January 24, 1944. "You see kids 10 and 12 years old playing tag in the streets, then about dusk start "pimping" for their whores. Kids seven or eight bumming cigarettes to trade for food. Of course there is almost nothing here, the Germans have stripped the country."

Lecce was an enterprising place, though, and the locals knew exactly how to exploit two of the airmens' biggest weaknesses, wine and women, for cold hard cash of course. A bottle of homemade vino sold for ten cents a bottle. The size of the container made no difference in the price. The other product was more expensive and in even more demand. Prostitution and armaments manufacture share the dubious distinction of being the principal commercial beneficiaries of 20th Century warfare. Nowhere was the former more evident than in Lecce.

A whorehouse sat on just about every corner. Sadly, it was the only way many of the women were able to keep their families fed. Although prostitution itself was never an issue with the army, VD was. The military brass did everything in its power to harangue the men about the ravages of venereal disease. Yet, an endless stream of lectures and graphic films on the subject fell mostly on deaf ears.

By early 1944, VD was rampant throughout much of the theatre in Italy. So much so, that Allied Command had become alarmed. At one point, British medical officers reported they were treating 40,000 cases of gonorrhea and syphilis every month. The fight for democracy seemed in mortal danger of collapse. The situation demanded immediate attention. In Lecce, Joe and some of his buddies were pressed into service in the never ending war against VD.

"The military police would order a bunch of us into the back of a truck," he recalls. "They would take us to one of the "houses" where a couple of provost marshals would knock on the front door while the rest of us would be posted at the back."

The routine was always the same. With the first loud knock on the front door, out would come a bevy of young "ladies" by the back, where Joe and his pals would catch them like flies. The women were herded into trucks for a quick trip to the base clinic where blood work would be done. If a hooker tested positive, her picture would be posted in the town square for all to see. The soldiers were on official notice to stay away from these individuals or face arrest. Joe had to laugh every time one of the women tried to negotiate her freedom with promises of "special favors." No doubt about it, Joe found himself fighting two fronts in this war.

Bad weather kept the 98th grounded for much of early March. But, by the middle of the month, things began to look up. Thirty-three B-24s were able to struggle off the mud sodden runways to bomb a submarine pen at Toulon, France on the afternoon of the 14th. This time it was Joe's turn to fly with a more experienced crew. Assigned to the nose turret, he hated every minute of it.

"Imagine yourself sitting on a chair inside a glass bubble and being hurled through thin air without being able to see the rest of the aircraft," he says. "That was me!" The mission was a success and they didn't run into any serious flak or fighters. As miserable as he was, Joe at least considered himself fortunate that day. But he swore he would never fly "up front" again, and he didn't. A few days later, a much happier Joe was back with his old crew on a run to one of the more famous battlefronts of the war— Cassino. The mission, once again, would be in support of Allied ground troops.

Without the capture of the heavily fortified German positions in the town of Cassino, there could be no Allied advance on Rome and no linking up with the bridgehead at Anzio. Tactical bombing was the only answer. A month before, the Allies had dropped leaflets warning the Germans that the monastery on Monte Cassino would be bombed, and then carried out their threat on one of the shrines of early medieval Christian culture. Over the objections of the Americans, the British believed the Germans were using the abbey as an observation post to survey their ground troops.

Although the Benedictine monastery was reduced to rubble, the Allied infantry assault later that day failed to dislodge the German defenders from the slopes. On March 15th, several heavy bomber groups of the 15th Air Force, including the 98th in Lecce, were tasked with finishing the job. This time the target would be the town of Cassino itself, with hundreds of bombers to be deployed in an all out effort. If everything went according to plan, a hole would be blasted through the enemy line through which

Allied troops would pour and advance up the boot of Italy.

From the moment the first bombs lurched out of the lead ship, pure bedlam exploded in the skies over Cassino. Two hundred and seventy-five B-24s and B-17s, along with another 200 medium bombers from the 12th Air Force, zigzagged back and forth through the heavy flak at all altitudes. Joe was thunderstruck. He had never before witnessed so many planes in one place at one time. He was amazed that the bombers didn't end up dropping their payloads on each other. He was glad Fred Streicher was at the controls.

After five long hours of mass confusion, strike photos indicated the Allied bomb bursts had completely covered the prime target. Cassino was demolished and Joe was happy to be alive. However, an army buddy of his from Norfolk was anything but happy with the results. According to Francis Jackman, who was on the ground with the infantry that day, some of the bombers had missed their mark and American soldiers died as a result.

"Francis has cursed me to this day," says Joe. "He insists that some of us missed the town altogether and hit our own troops in the pull back position just south of the target."

Joe doesn't buy that argument completely, believing, instead, that if some of their soldiers died by friendly fire, it had to be the result of them moving back into the target zone before the all clear signal was given. Pilots and navigators were always painfully aware of the implications of even the slightest error during a tactical operation like this, especially when the target was obscured by smoke from their own strikes. Nevertheless, bomber crews were constantly haunted by such possibilities, and therefore Joe could never be quite sure about his friend's claims. (After the war, the U.S. Army did determine that bombs from the heavies had in fact fallen among Allied troops but blame was not assessed.)

Mission followed mission for *Maggie's Drawers* in the final two weeks of March 1944. Airdromes, marshalling yards and targets of opportunity from Italy to Austria and Bulgaria were hit. Fires with blinding flashes and columns of black smoke followed Joe and his crew everywhere. By the end of the month, the 98th Bomb Group had reached a milestone, its 200th mission.

By this time the 98th had dropped more than 14 and a half million pounds of bombs, initiated nearly 4,000 sorties and accounted for 271 enemy aircraft shot down, with an added 71 planes probably destroyed. But, not all of their missions had been spectacular. In fact they were the exception. The more a crew went out, the more each operation began to feel like the one before. This is an unusual epitaph, even for a war, but it did happen to many crews, including Joe's. The airmen found the bomber offensive to be an impersonal sort of war and monotonous in its own peculiar way. Day after day, as weather and resources permitted, the heavies went out, dropped their deadly load and returned home. No single mission was ever decisive. Instead, they were long, tedious and frustrating ventures more often than not.

The grind of everyday combat also manifested itself in the form of flying fatigue. Airmen were subjected to the same stresses as their counterparts on the ground and at sea. But in addition, the psychological effects of impersonal hazards faced by the air crews, such as anoxia, critically low temperatures causing frostbite, toothaches from breathing too much pure oxygen, and not even being able to take a leak while the ship rattled their kidneys, took their toll over time. A bomber was better than a muddy slit trench, but not by much.

In order to deal with the constant stress, Joe and the others constantly sought out all sorts of diversion. The army often obliged them by bringing in the big stars of stage, screen and radio from back home. Red Skelton was a favorite. So were such names as Joe E. Brown and John Garfield.

For an extra special treat, the 98th would send out a stripped down B-24 to Cairo, Egypt for supplies once a month. *Maggie's Drawers* was next on the roster and Joe looked forward to the break and the chance to buy some Three Feathers whiskey that he could smuggle back and sell for a tidy profit. The chance to get a little action on the black market always appealed to him.

Steyr, the thousand year old iron town in upper Austria that was bombed on April 2, 1944.

There were other outlets for the more culturally minded among them. They could always go to the Italian Opera House in Lecce to catch a production of the *Barber of Seville*. For the rest, like Joe's crewmate, William Koller, there was gambling. Wherever you looked, in a corner of the barracks, under a tent flap or inside the mess hall, there was always a poker game going on. Despite the distractions, reality was never very far away. There was always the next mission. Always.

Steyr, Austria. It was home to the rolling stock of modern industrial warfare. One of Hitler's ballbearing factories was next on the 98's hit list. The heavies had already tried, and failed twice to bomb it. The first time, 40 Liberators were sent out. The next attempt was even more massive with 234 bombers. Each time foul weather put a quick end to their plans. To make matters worse, visibility was so bad on the second try that two bombers, 20 men, were lost in a mid-air collision. While two other bomber groups had managed to do some collateral damage to the Austrian town five weeks earlier, the Steyr ballbearing factory remained a festering disappointment for the 98th. Joe had a disquieting feeling deep inside his gut about his next target. The last time he felt this way was the day he stood before the ponderous steel gates guarding the entrance to Fort Devens, Massachusetts, the fateful day he signed up.

CHAPTER SIX

Palmsonntag

When the blast of war blows in our ears,
Then imitate the action of the tiger;
Stiffen the sinews, summon up the blood,
Disguise fair nature with hard-favored rage.

William Shakespeare
Henry V (1598)

A grey wisp of dawn pierced the fragile serenity at the USAAF base in Lecce on April 2, 1944. Another eerie game of Russian roulette was afoot. It was Palm Sunday, 0600, the usual sickening hour before flight. Sleep-starved crews had already scrambled into their smelly flight suits and gathered up their oxygen masks, parachutes and Mae Wests from the supply hut. Escape kits too, for extra insurance.

Fred Streicher and his officers were already off to the briefing hut by the time Joe had settled into his duties deep inside the dingy bowels of *Maggie's Drawers*. With delicate precision, he checked each bomb rack to make sure the shackles were properly secured. He deftly ran a knowing hand along the gun controls and ammunition belts until he was satisfied. Nothing, absolutely nothing, was ever allowed to escape his scrutiny when it came to the safety of his ship and crew.

Joe chatted animatedly with the rest of the enlisted men as he stooped from his six foot frame to double check the spare crate of bullets propped up against the bulkhead. The air of contrived casualness that punctuated the banter helped calm his nerves. For others, though, inner thoughts overwhelmed any attempt at small talk.

Even with 51 hours of combat time under his belt, Joe was still overwhelmed by the pronounced smell that assailed his nostrils every time he climbed aboard. The ship had a tang like nothing else he had ever known, a foul combination of oil, grease, hydraulics, engine exhaust and dank hard steel. If fear had a smell, Joe had surely come to know it well.

Yet, he managed a playful smile when his attention turned to a carton of K-rations stowed by the waist window. It reminded

Joseph L. Maloney, 21 years old, 1944 in formal uniform after his return from the war. Note the 15th AF Badge.

him of the many times he and his buddies used to throw their boxes of spare food out of the waist windows at the end of every mission. His eyes were drawn across the leaden sky to a small clearing at the end of the runway. That's where the locals always hung out for a hand-out. A returning B-24 was always a welcome sight to the hungry Italians.

The bomber crews were only too happy to oblige, since it saved them time from cleaning up the aircraft back at the hardstand. Unfortunately, for those below, the airmen often got carried away with their generosity. Along with their leftover rations, they also liked to serve up something else in brown paper bags while on the final approach. Joe couldn't help but laugh when he remembered the look of shock on the faces of those unlucky enough to grab one of the surprise packages. As he recalled, they were never amused to find that they were holding nothing more than the messy results of someone's disposable john.

"We used to get a lot of fists shaken at us for that one," quips Joe. "I guess we did it to break the tension of the mission."

"Hey! We've got to go to the warehouse to get our new secret weapon." The distant voice of radio operator John Reilly snapped Joe from the narrow dimension of his faraway thoughts.

"It's something called *Window*," John blithered on good-naturedly. Although many airmen like Joe had never heard of Window before, it was in fact the earliest form of radar jamming device to be used in the war. Introduced by RAF Bomber Command in December 1942, Window, sometimes called Chaff by the Americans, consisted of thousands of pieces of metallic strips, colored black on one side and cut into various lengths. The strips, like icicles on a Christmas tree, reflected ground based radar signals when thrown over the target, blinding the German radar screens, thus preventing the enemy from pinpointing the approaching bombers.

The more Joe heard about this new technical marvel, the more he was convinced that the enemy's fighters and radar directed anti-aircraft fire might be rendered ineffective for the rest of the war. He felt even better after being told his crew was due for some well deserved R&R on the Isle of Capri off Naples the following week. It would be their first break from active duty since coming overseas and he looked forward to it. This just might not be such a bad day after all.

Only one thing really irritated Joe that morning. The cook had over slept and that meant dry toast and black coffee instead of his usual hot meal. Was it a bad omen? Maybe, he thought. But, then he figured dinner would taste even better when he got back later that day. Had he known more about Window, he would have made sure his stomach was more than satisfied that morning.

The wily Germans had quickly learned how to cope very effectively with this Allied counterweapon. In many cases, Window actually helped the enemy detect the target area in advance since the strips were dropped just before an attack. The concentration of "snow" on their radar screens showed the German gunners precisely where the bombers were. All they had to do was aim their big 88s at the center of the "snow" field and it was open season on anybody who got in the way. Although the Allies were slowly winning the air war, they were reminded from time to time that German ingenuity and tenacity were still formidable opponents, even by Spring 1944. The so called "milk run" would remain principally a myth for most bomber crews, including Joe's.

In early 1944, Lieutenant General Ira C. Eaker, Air Chief in the Mediterranean Theatre, revealed just how badly the air war had been going. He confessed to losing more than 20,750 men over the previous 12 months. The combat crew strength of the 15th Air Force was about 20,000 men. The inescapable conclusion was that the 15th had lost 100% of its strength, including the staggering loss of 2,050 heavy bombers, all in a single combat year. And that wasn't all.

In the first few months of 1944, the total number of B-17s lost or damaged reached the dismal total of 4,233, or 13%. Of this number, 566 were shot down. The B-24, because of its greater vulnerability, was employed on fewer missions, sustaining a total loss or damage of 1,006, of which 210 were downed. The odds of an individual airman like Joe surviving each new mission grew worse with every passing day. There was now less than a one in three chance of a crewman getting through a raid alive.

Steyr weighed heavily on Joe's mind as he went about his pre-flight checks that early April morning. A heavy veil of doom and gloom hung over him like a cold wet blanket. No matter how hard he tried, he could not shake the negative feeling that he was about to go to his own funeral. Determined not to put his crew at risk because of his faltering nerve, Joe finally decided to book off sick. To his great relief, John Reilly had the same idea. There was just no way they were going to try their luck against the same target for the third time in a row. Joe wasn't the superstitious kind, but, the number three spooked the hell out of him that morning.

While Joe and John tried to figure out a way to make their intentions known, the rest of the crew continued to load Window or were kept busy with some last minute checks at their battle stations. Then something out of the ordinary happened. At precisely 0710 hours, Streicher and his officers rushed back from the briefing hut, and, without a second's delay or a word of explanation, they sealed the doors, revved up the engines and taxied for take off. The mission's start had been bumped up. German spies must have been working overtime, Joe figured with a deep sigh. He knew he had just kissed his plans to stay home good-bye.

"So much for plan A," he muttered as *Maggie's Drawers* roared into flight along with 33 other B-24s.

As the clutch of Libs droned towards its predetermined bombing altitude, the temperature inside *Maggie's Drawers* plunged two degrees centigrade every thousand feet she climbed, an out and out torment for every single crew member. As altitude increased, they became less efficient. Their ears bothered them and head congestion often caused severe pain. Ignoring their discomfort, they soldiered on. An hour into the mission, Joe's 415th Squadron rendezvoused with the 449th and the 450th from other bases in Italy at 3,000 feet and continued on course. It was only then that Fred Streicher officially informed his crew that Steyr would be the day's target. There was no turning back now, despite Joe's nagging misgivings about his tenth mission. But, once committed, he decided to make the best of it. He would not let his buddies down. Nor was he about to jeopardize the stellar reputation of his bomber group either.

Officially activated as a Heavy Bombardment Group on February 3, 1942 at MacDill Field in Florida, the five squadrons of the 98th became operational in the Mediterranean Theatre on July 25 the same year, when the first air echelon arrived in Ramat David, near Haifa in Palestine. The group flew its first mission exactly a week later, hitting Rommel's tank repair installations at Mersa Matruh, Egypt. The 98th continued to operate from bases in Palestine until November 11, when it began a long series of forward movements in the wake of the victorious British 8th Army at El Alamein.

By this time, the group had a number of impressive missions under its belt, including shipping strikes and attacks over Crete and Greece. It destroyed thousands of tons of supplies and valuable oil belonging to the badly pressed Axis forces. The 98th was particularly proud of its participation in *"Tital Wave,"* the epic low level raid against what Winston Churchill called the "taproot of German might," the Ploesti oil refinery in Romania. On August 1, 1943, 164 B-24s from several combat groups hit the target, some flying at no more than 20 feet off the ground. Fifty-four bombers didn't return and two out of five airmen never came back. Those who did were never the same, as Joe recalled. To him, they were like zombies.

The 98th's efforts in the Libyan, Tunisian, Sicilian and Italian campaigns earned it nine Battle Stars. More citations would come its way but only at great cost when the 98th began looking north of the Alps after grabbing a toe hold in southern Italy, first at Brindisi, then Manduria and finally Lecce. Joe had a big tradition to uphold.

As *Maggie's Drawers* reached the 10,000 foot mark, Joe snapped on his oxygen mask and plugged in his flight suit before hunkering down for the long and tedious five hour journey to the target. The flight plan would take the phalanx of bombers on a northerly course across the Adriatic Sea, up over the Alps and then on to the thousand year old iron town in upper Austria.

At 1049 the formation rendezvoused with its fighter escorts, P-38 Lightnings and P-47 Thunderbolts, at 12,000 feet. They would provide the much needed target penetration cover. The new long-range drop tank P-51s crucial for the lumbering bombers on such long missions over enemy territory were absent. The Mustangs were probably needed somewhere else that day. They would have to make do with what they had. Luck of the draw.

Joe and his crew-mates struggled as best they could against the relentless vibration and the fitful evasive maneuvers of the heavily laden *Maggie's Drawers*. Finally, the formation leveled off at 20,000 feet, their bombing altitude. The race to get the mission over with was on. Cold, lonely and frightened, with nothing but time on their hands, the airmen could do little more at this point than ponder their miserable existence before all hell broke loose over the target. That is, if the enemy let them get that far.

Joe Maloney and Clarence Jensen, Lecce, Italy, March 1944. Clarence was the engineer on the B-24.

Fred Streicher and the flight crew donned their flak jackets and helmets. At the back of the ship, the gunners, with the exception of Joe of course, already had theirs on. Constantly scanning the blue void for enemy fighters in the form of some distant specks of dirt while maintaining radio silence, only added to the numbing tedium.

Riding along the edge of the frigid and rarefied air of the stratosphere, white majestic condensation trails marked the paths of the refulgent Liberators. It would have been a pretty sight, had any of the airmen taken the time to notice. Among their many duties, the crews were far too busy watching for ground activity. When visibility was good, they looked for marshalling yards, shipping traffic and industrial smoke. Anything they felt might be of use to army intelligence was duly noted and recorded for later missions.

With glacial determination, Joe reassured himself, over and over again, that no mission, not even this one, could possibly be as hellish as the one he had been ordered to go on a month earlier. At least this time, there was some comfort in knowing that he was not on a suicide mission right from the start.

"In early March, we were ordered to fly to northern Germany, a tremendous distance from our base in southern Italy," he recalls. "We were told we would have enough fuel to reach the target and get half way back. We would also have no fighter escorts once deep inside Germany."

For the 280 men assigned this grim task, the message was as clear as it was chilling. They were told that coming back was secondary and that if no one returned and the target were destroyed, the mission would be considered a success. A cold shiver ran down his back, as Joe vividly recalled every dreadful detail of that terrible morning.

"We tied our boots to our parachute harnesses, something we never did," he says. "We took our sidearms, and shook hands with the ground crew, sure signs we were not coming back."

The men went through their usual pre-flight inspections, and, for the first time that Joe could remember, the B-24s were topped off with fuel as they idled at the end of the runway waiting for takeoff. The small amount of extra gasoline would make no difference but Joe thought it was a nice gesture by the ground crew anyway. At the eleventh hour, however, their luck changed. Failing to break out of some heavy cloud cover at 11,000 feet, the bombers could not get into formation. Bad weather, which they had always cursed, had just saved their hides.

It was often said that there were no atheists in the war-torn skies of Europe. They were probably right. Joe always had a talk with God during times like these. When his suicide mission to northern Germany was scrubbed, he knew his prayers had been answered. He also got results on one other prayer as well.

No longer relegated to the perilous "Tail End Charlie" slot, *Maggie's Drawers* was now flying the more protected number six position in the second "v." The whole crew was emboldened by this turn of events. After a B-24 up front was forced to return to base early, Streicher eased his ship into the number three spot, left wing, first "v" element in the second wave. They were on their way with at least some hint of security.

For some reason, Joe didn't knew why, Waldo Akers was not aboard that day. Instead, a new guy, Ed O'Connor, had the nose turret position. It was his first mission, and, thinking about his own nightmare when he had been up there, Joe felt sorry for him. He also felt nervous about the rookie. What if O'Connor froze at the worst possible moment? Joe's skepticism lingered as he returned his steely gaze towards the infinite blue sky.

Three of the Liberators were forced to turn back as the formation crossed the border into Austria. It couldn't have come at a worst time. Every enemy fighter would now be spoiling for a fight. But, as usual, the rest of the group pressed on.

Fred Streicher knew the Germans already had a fix on his position by now. As soon as the bombers left Italy, enemy radar locked on and the Luftwaffe defenders, mostly the rough and ready ME 109s, ME110s, FW 190s and Junkers 88s, were scrambled from their bases all over occupied southern Europe. The point of interception could take place any time now. Every crewman in the formation was on full alert for hostile aircraft.

Joe could never get over just how quickly a fighter could pounce out of nowhere and go tearing through a formation. With little or no warning, their blazing 20mm cannons could punch countless deadly rounds into an unsuspecting bomber. Attack after attack would come with groups of two, three or four, sometimes as many as nine enemy fighters abreast. Then, just as suddenly, it would be over as the Luftwaffe pilots turned their attention to the crippled stragglers for an easy kill. Only the lucky bomber crews would live to fight another day.

The muffled chatter of heavy machine gun fire erupted from Joe's ship. It scared the crap out of him until he realized the crew was just making sure their defensive positions were in top fighting form. They were, except for one of the twin 50s on John Reilly's top turret. It was jammed. On top of his attempt to book off sick that morning, Reilly was not having a good day. A decision had to be made about the status of the ship in light of this new problem.

Joe was in a sticky predicament. As armorer gunner, he was responsible for fixing the problem. Yet, every man had to keep his post while over enemy territory. The rules were clear on this point. There were no exceptions. The repairs would have to wait, or *Maggie's Drawers* would have to turn back.

Normally, a finicky gun would be more than enough reason for a B-24 pilot to hightail it for home. But their more secure spot in the formation, along with their unflinching loyalty to the group, convinced Streicher and the rest of the crew to press on. Besides, one gun out of ten was no big deal. Or so they thought.

The formation, now lead by 155 bombers from the 455th Group, grew to over 280 B-24s and B-17s by the time *Maggie's Drawers* droned deeper into Austria. The large number of bombers meant only one thing. Steyr would be a major strike. It also meant the target would be defended to the hilt.

The 30 Liberators in Joe's 415th Squadron, tucked away in the middle of the armada, carried incendiaries in their bellies. The lead squad had demolition bombs aboard. It would be their job to blast the target to pieces in one colossal strike. Joe's squadron had the follow-up task of burning the rubble left behind. Even the chaos of high tech destruction demanded an orderly sequence, Joe mused as he felt a familiar rumble.

Maggie's Drawers began to stagger as she bore into the snarling jaws of a flak field, nine interminable minutes before the release point. The match with death was on. Thundering concussions from the flak bursts bucked the ratchety ship as Joe fought for control of his guns and his nerves. Minutes crept by like hours under the relentless buffeting.

At 1223 hours, the 415th reached its IP, made a left hand turn and closed in on the target on an axis of 340 degrees at 21,500 feet. They were now committed to the bomb run. Only three more minutes to go. It might as well have been 3 years. The sky was a panoply of explosions. Joe scanned the blemished horizon for any sign of enemy fighters.

Just as the hail of black death suddenly fell silent from the belching 88s below, a swarm of Nazi fighters weighted in at twelve o'clock high. Brimming with fire power, the Luftwaffe stood its ground between the lead strike force and the target. The bomber crews were now caught in a deadly game of chicken. They knew they were easy prey, but there wasn't a thing they could do about it. Like the rest of the formation, *Maggie's Drawers* had to fly a precarious course, straight and level and at a constant speed. Any sudden move or deviation from the prescribed route would mess up the bomb run. This, above all, had to be avoided in spite of the terrible risk.

Joe watched in disgust as the waist gunners in neighboring ships threw out their last boxes of Window. He cursed, knowing the crinkly tinfoil had not made one bit of difference. Within seconds, a hundred marauding ME-109s and 210s, FW-190s and rocket spewing JU-88s started to throw everything they had into the middle of the lead group at point blank range. Just beyond the maelstrom, a clutch of P-38 and P-47 escorts disappeared from Streicher's view. They were probably battling it out on the other side of the target where the leading edge of bombers was already beginning to rally away. Streicher and the others maintained their heading, knowing they too were about to be delivered thru the gates of Hell.

It didn't take long for the ravaged second wave to come completely apart. In a primordial vision of Hell, the sky over Steyr turned into a bedlam of bombers swarming in all directions, many riddled with gaping holes, some with smoking engines and others with their dead and dying on board. The 15th Air Force was caught in the clutches of a deadly battle, the heaviest resistance it had ever encountered in the war. Defiantly, Joe's squadron, or what was left of it, soldiered on to its single minded objective, oblivious to the aerial wasteland of their hell-bent intrusion.

Four miles below, the air-raid sirens of Steyr were wailing "a horrible up and down swelling sound" as if in a shouting match with the chaos above. The bombers had triggered the alarms all over upper Austria. Listening posts and acoustic detectors reported the approaching formation as soon as it had crossed the Julian Alps by way of Slovenija in northern Yugoslavia.

Just as Streicher and his crew had suspected all along, the German Air Defense was already in high gear as the leading edge of the bomber fleet poured across Croatian airspace, in advance of the Austrian border. Young German pilots swung into action from an airfield in Annabichl, near Klagenfurt, well to the south of Steyr. The enemy squadron was quickly joined by more fighters from occupied upper Italy. Together, they lay in wait. An excited voice had already announced the first bomber sightings from the command station of the German Air Defense.

"Hello, here air base Klagenfurt. Hello, planes..."

Then, after a short break, again, the same voice.

"Hello, do you listen? Two hundred and fifty planes. Type Flying Fortress. Type Liberator. Destination north."

The ominous lament of the air-raid sirens shortly before noon had startled Steyr's worshippers. They hurriedly ran from their places of worship. Many of the children, and even some of the grownups, were still clutching bunches of pussy willows in their trembling hands as they poured into the streets. Until the mad rush had begun, they had been celebrating Palmsonntag, Palm Sunday, a special time in the lives of all Christians, as they always had, in peace and quiet.

The budding flora they carried with them symbolized the triumphant entry of Jesus into Jerusalem and the beginning of redemption. For Steyr, during this Palmsonntag at least, there would be no time for the atonement of sins. As the worshipers scurried into underground shelters that boasted gas locks, a complete water plant, toilets and operating rooms, every man, woman and child prayed the bombers would not unleash another torrent of destruction. Remarkably, this small Austrian town had experienced little in the way of war throughout its first millennium. There were a few skirmishes during the peasant uprisings in some distant past, and there was some minor public disorder during the Reformation. The Turks had even invaded Steyr without a fight. Otherwise, it had been a peaceful town, until 1939, when it became an industrial center for Hitler's war machine. On a cold winter's day in early 1944, the Allies had come for the first time. Punishment was swift and decisive. It was a day Steyr would never forget.

On the morning of February 23, 30 planes finally reached their target and dropped 288 demolition bombs, some right in the middle of the embattled enclave; 15 people died and 55 were injured. Steyr was stunned. Since 1939 residents had been preparing for such a day by sandbagging their basement windows, learning how to fight the impact of incendiary bombs and taking first aid lessons. Even gas masks were kept at the ready. But nothing had prepared them for this day, nor for what was to follow. After the dust had settled, Erna Sohnle, a vivacious 19 year old factory worker, asked the question burning on everybody's lips.

"Will they come back?" she wondered aloud.

Cheering up, she patted her girl friend's shoulder and tried to answer her own question.

"Surely that was a coincidence. Nobody gets hurt in Steyr."

The next afternoon, 87 heavy bombers, stationed in Foggio, just north of Lecce, came with her answer. Two hundred and ten people in Steyr died that day. Three hundred and seventy one suffered severe injuries. Over a thousand residents lost their homes. Despite some fierce protection from their P-38 and P-47 escorts, the 15th Air Force lost 17 bombers in the skies over Steyr. It was a dark day all around.

In the weeks to follow, the factories in Steyr that escaped destruction were filled with fatigued, emaciated men and women operating welders, lathes and heavy milling machines. Like always, the children were sent to school. And, like always, the shops opened at 7:00 a.m. sharp, though there was little to offer. The brave faces of Steyr masked a very deep wound.

The shell shocked survivors were forbidden from writing about their experiences. The Reich exercised absolute control over all information it didn't want getting into the hands of its hard pressed troops. However, the bombing victims would not forget the terror that had visited them with such punishing force that day. How could they forget the ear splitting roar from the hundreds of bomber engines that drowned out the furious bark of the flak guns? Nor would they ever forget the whistling scream of the bombs.

The walls of their air-raid shelters shook from the rain of steel. Children clung terrified to their mother's necks. Within a matter of minutes, 1200 heavy demolition bombs rained into the town. Each explosion ripped a deep wound, collapsing walls and sinking houses into the ground. Trees broke like matches; thousands of panes of glass burst, while a chaos of bricks, shrapnel and power lines splattered across the streets. Fires flared. With morbid fascination, eyes that had lost all expression were drawn to the horror of sudden changes in air pressure whenever a bomb went off. Those too close to the point of impact felt a strange gurgling sound as their blood erupted in their lungs and spewed from their mouths, noses and ears.

After the last wave of bombers disappeared, an immense cloud of dust and smoke rose over Steyr. Ascending to several thousand feet, the dark shroud of destruction concealed the entire Alpine range. The flak guns fell silent as did the last of the dying, Erna Sohnle, among them. Neighbors pulled her broken body from the basement of a building where she had been hiding, no doubt praying this day would never come.

Particularly disappointing for the 15th Air Force was the fact that the raid itself had caused so little direct damage to the prime target—Steyr's ballbearing plant. Three bombs did hit the grinding department. More important were hits which interrupted the power supply to the plant for the next two weeks. But, this wasn't good enough. The heavy American bombers would have to come back. The next time, though, a much better prepared Steyr would have a little surprise in store for the winged warriors. Steyr was bent on revenge.

CHAPTER SEVEN

The Sky Is Falling
Farewell happy fields
Where joy forever dwells,
Hail horrors, hail!

> *John Milton*
> *Paradise Lost (1667)*

"Pilot to bombardier." The voice of Fred Streicher crackled over the ship's intercom as he shot a defiant scowl at the flock of enemy fighters still blocking his path. He had already made up his mind. There was no way he was going to back off and run from a good fight. Not after coming this far.

"Target coming up," he continued in a remarkably calm voice.

"Thirty seconds to release," came Clark Fetterman's terse acknowledgment, as he reached down to his control stand and gingerly placed his right thumb and forefinger on the cold toggle switch.

The young bombardier pulled in a deep breath and held it. He waited. Then he waited some more as he kept a sharp eye on the lead plane, only faintly visible now through the haze of battle.

"Bombs away," Fetterman called out a second later, sweat beading on his forehead in spite of the severe cold.

Maggie's Drawers lurched slightly as the heavy bundles of incendiaries tumbled out and wobbled momentarily in the freezing blast of the slipstream before disappearing. Joe watched the deadly payload shower into the smoke-choked air below, another reminder that at least he had the best seat in the house. It was the only perk of the job.

Destruction was heavy at the Daimler-Puch Waelzlogerwesr Ball Bearing plant in Steyr, Austria after the Allied bombing raid of April 2, 1944. Joe's plane was shot down during this mission.

As he fixed his gaze on the sinking bomb stream, Joe couldn't help but notice there was something odd about the obscured target. There was way too much smoke, and it was too light in color. Little did he know that Steyr's defenders had come prepared this time.

After its withering drubbing in February, the city's Ground Command was determined never to let it happen again. So, they came up with a clever way to better protect themselves. Fog. Barrels, from which white chemical fumes would be released, were located on the hilly outskirts of Steyr, at the Tabor on the Ennsleite in Kleinabermein, on the Dachsberg, and on the Christkindlleite. On April 2, their experiment in survival was put to the test. The fog was released just in advance of the bombers approach. Within minutes, the steep gables of the old town sunk into a surging artificial sea of white mist. Only the two factory chimneys and the top of the town church were towering out.

However, their clever ruse almost backfired. Just as the bombers appeared overhead, the bank of fog was carried off by a light easterly breeze. The nearby countryside was covered, but Steyr and its ball bearing factory were left out in the open. The defenders were dumbfounded. Then, something very unexpected happened. Witnesses on the ground claim the Allied commander of the scout plane, who directed the bombers to their objective, dropped his markers into the outskirts of Steyr. The rest of the armada followed. This small error, they say, saved the day. The bulk of the bombs fell into the great mist, transforming the pristine rural landscape into a morass of smoldering craters. The peasants were terrified as smoke floated over their burning farms and forests. While the folks of Steyr thanked their lucky stars, the 15th Air Force did not come away entirely empty handed. Several of their bombs did slam into the ball bearing mill at the edge of town, which sank into a roiling inferno of flame and smoke.

Five miles above the burning and broken earth, Streicher banked hard left for a reciprocal course home. Lurking on the other side of the target, 100 or so FW-190s, ME-109s and twin-engine JU-88s had something else in mind for them.

"They swooped in over us and started dropping butterfly bombs into our rallying away point." Joe says. At the same time, Joe caught a glimpse of some ME-110s darting out of the black horizon from directly behind his ship at 6 o'clock high. He started counting. Two. Four. Six. His skin crawled. Eight. Nine of them abreast! In the throes of a steep bank, *Maggie's Drawers* was a sitting duck.

Just as he thought the situation couldn't get any worse, Joe heard the plaintive voice of Fred Streicher in his headphones. It was a curt message. "JU-88s at 10 o'clock low and closing in!"

The ME-110s had been a decoy! *Maggie's Drawers* was primed for the kill. The ship heaved as her tattered frame shuttered under the pounding sledgehammer blows of the 20mm shells. A split second later, a sickening rumble belched from deep inside the strickened ship.

"We're hit!" Streicher exclaimed, trying to force his voice to remain a lot calmer than he really was. "God Almighty," John Reilly yelled out, still struggling with his jammed gun as Joe said a quick prayer. Talking to God was always Joe's road map to sanity in the midst of insanity.

Minutes before this, Newbold Noyes Jr. had been enjoying a panoramic view from the flight deck of *Little Joe*. Aboard the lead ship in the third

A JU.88 captured by the Allies. A Junkers like this one shot down Joe's B-24. It was the Luftwaffe's most versatile aircraft.

box, the young war correspondent from the *Washington Sunday Star* was riding along by special permission of pilot, Lieutenant Mike Meger of Crivitz, Wisconsin. If Noyes had ever wondered how far he would go to get a good story, he now had his answer. He didn't know whether to thank Meger or curse him.

On Meger's left wing was "a good teammate in a fight," Noyes would later write. In fact the two Liberators were so close that he could see "the face of the man behind the waist gun grin in his helmet and oxygen mask." Noyes further observed: "the whole airplane seemed to bristle, challenging the sky around us. We'll call her Mary." His neighbor was none other than *Maggie's Drawers*.

At that moment, everything seemed right with the world. The Alps stretched out behind Noyes, their white mountain peaks shimmering in the brilliant midday sun. But dead ahead lay the satanic flak field that soon grabbed the young reporter by the throat as he watched bomber after bomber begin to cartwheel out of control and spin down to earth. He couldn't help but notice the heavies were taking an awful beating. "One bomber sheared off from the formation," he would write. "Something was on fire on one of the wings, a motor or a fuel tank. It went into a spin. It made five or six turns, then it broke in two just back of the center of the fuselage. The pieces fell in slow motion. We watched for parachutes but we could not see any." Seconds later, Noyes heard the agitated voice of Mike Meger on the intercom. "Pilot to nose gunner. For God's sake what about those planes coming in at 10 o'clock. Let 'em have it." Coming off the target, Meger had spotted half a dozen fighters coming right at him, launching their rockets. Noyes watched as "balls of fire" spewed from under their wings and tore into the loose formation. *Little Joe* was spared, but *Maggie's Drawers* was not so lucky. "Staggering, the battered ship held its position in the formation for a few minutes and then suddenly it was gone," Noyes scribbled in his notebook with a trembling hand. He couldn't believe how quickly "Mary" had simply vanished. The image of the waist gunner's smiling face now haunted him. He also felt a pang of guilt. Noyes was supposed to fly with Streicher that day, but by some fortuitous screwup he had ended up with Meger instead.

Mike Meger also felt the loss. He had been worried on the way up because nobody was beside him. When "Mary" showed up, he "smiled and waved to the boy flying her." It was good to see a fellow pilot share his lonely burden. But now, Meger would have to live with the torment of watching his friend "peeling off to the left and downward at a steep angle." Figuring "Mary" had had it, he turned to the job at hand, trying to get his own men back home alive. Meger would earn the Distinguished Flying Cross for his troubles.

Suddenly another Liberator spun out of control. Then another. And another. This was turning out to be a whole lot worse than Newbold Noyes could have ever imagined. A typical journalist, he wanted to go on a bombing raid to complete the picture of what life was really like for an air crew. "I had in mind a sort of nice easy "milk run" mission sort of a typical thing," he wrote his mother. "What I stepped into was the greatest running battle between bombers and enemy fighters in the history of Mediterranean warfare, a real colossal thing."

Censorship and transmission snarls delayed his story from getting out right away. Noyes finally told the whole story on the front page of the *Washington Sunday Star* a week later. He detailed just how badly the formation was chopped to pieces.

"All at once where there had been a fighter, there was a brilliant red flash from which the ship emerged spinning and burning. In the course of the battle, something hit the lead plane of the group on our right. The Liberator blew up, flying into pieces."

"Part of the bomber," his report continued, "probably a motor, struck the ship on its right, shearing off the nose just forward of the wing. The second plane went into a spin. One wing and part of its tail came off. The wreckage of the two planes fell on a third, which swerved sharply to the left out of its formation and a moment later started to spin. We could see this third ship all the way down. It did not disintegrate or burn, it simply spun to earth with every man still inside."

Death was taking no holiday and it took its toll on Noyes. In an April 8, 1944 letter to his mother, he explained further.

"At first, I thought I was just scared, and sat down on the floor to think things over. We'd been on oxygen for about an hour, and I thought probably that was what was making me feel funny. Automatically, I reached down to feel the oxygen hose leading to my mask and the thing wasn't there! There was a joint in the hose about six inches from the mask, and it had pulled apart at that point."

"I frantically poked the engineer, and waved the loose piece of hose under his nose. He dove for the rest of the hose which was laying on the floor, and very quickly screwed the two ends together again. When we got back, I told the flight surgeon about this and he said 'Hell, that wasn't lack of oxygen that made you pass out, you just plain fainted.'"

"Now that I think back on it," Noyes concluded in his letter to home, " I'm inclined to agree with him. I think I just thought to myself 'I'm a goner,' and started to pass out by the power of suggestion."

Although *Maggie's Drawers* had spun down at a sharp angle, Streicher and Morrell managed to level out, while the rest of the crew scrambled to come up with a damage report. What they found was not encouraging. But, nobody was hurt, and, for the moment at least, they were out of the fray. A shocked hush fell over the ship as the enormity of their situation began to sink in. "The JU-88s had come at us at an odd angle," Joe says. "At ten o'clock low it meant they had to climb during their attack, sacrificing speed, something they never did." Joe figured the German pilots probably gambled on the B-24s' blind spot. They flew low enough to keep out of range of O'Connor's guns in the nose turret. And, hanging down in his goldfish bowl behind the bombbay, Art Fleming had his back to them, thinking an attack would come the usual way, from the rear. Likewise, the top, tail and waist guns were equally useless.

"We didn't get a single shot at them," Joe says slightly exasperated. The Junkers slammed at least two rockets into the ship's belly. In all the noise and confusion, Joe couldn't be sure of the count. It didn't matter anyway. They were just as wounded. *Maggie's Drawers* was also stitched from end to end with machine gunfire. She was not a pretty sight. Shrapnel had completely taken out two of her engines. A third one was racing out of control.

The pungent smell of cordite waffed through the bomber as Streicher pulled the throttle back on the wounded engine and feathered the runaway prop. He couldn't take a chance on the props getting stuck in the flight position. That would make them windmill out of control and slow them down something fierce.

Only one engine, number three right inboard, continued to deliver full power. A lucky break because it fed most of the ship's hydraulic systems, including flaps, bomb bay doors, landing gear and the Sperry automatic pilot. *Maggie's Drawers* could fly if Streicher could get enough power. A big if.

There was one other problem. Joe was the first to realize it because of his vantage point. The right wing fuel tank was spewing a huge vapor trail of gasoline. A single tracer bullet from one of their guns would turn the sky around them into a huge fireball. It meant the ship's entire starboard flank was exposed to attack with no way of defending it.

At the moment, though, Streicher and Morrell were more worried about their air speed. The Liberator, derided as *"The Flying Coffin"* by its detractors in best of circumstances, had little or no glide capability because of its large fuselage to small wing ratio. Even the official B-24 handbook warned pilots that it could not fly on one engine alone. Streicher's crew was determined to prove the experts wrong.

As *Maggie's Drawers* fell farther and farther behind, other bomber crews could only watch, transfixed by the torment of not being able to lend a hand. They had to stay within the relative protection of their formation, or what was left of it, for a fighting chance to get back home. Richard Parke was deeply saddened. Flying off the target at 200 miles per hour indicated air speed in another B-24, the flight engineer saw *Maggie's Drawers* "remain in its number three position approximately two to three minutes with gasoline spouting from a damaged engine before falling back and out of sight."

Aboard another B-24, tail gunner Clarence Laidlaw was a bit more optimistic. "I saw the ship fall back and low in the formation. I continued to watch until we were pretty close to the coast. It dropped far behind the formation and down to about 10,000 feet. From what I observed during the pursuit attacks this ship was left entirely alone by the enemy. I last saw it coming toward the coast of Yugoslavia, but it didn't seem to be losing any more altitude." Ball gunner Roy Anthony had a view of the action from yet another bomber. "I saw the ship falling behind with an engine on fire. I turned to fire at the fighters and later looked for the ship but it was nowhere in sight."

Fred Streicher struggled feverishly to keep *Maggie's Drawers* as level as possible. He trimmed the nose down ever so slightly to gain a bit of precious air speed. More than anything, he and Morrell wanted to maintain altitude long enough to get their wounded bird to Switzerland. The crew had often talked about using the neutral country as a safe harbor in case of trouble. That idea was soon nixed. They were losing too much altitude to try to get over the Alps. They would have to try something else.

The mood inside the aircraft grew bleaker. Deep inside enemy territory, alone, with no formation or fighter escorts, and with no place to hide, the crew fell silent, trying desperately to think of a way, any way, to turn death into a fighting chance to live. Joe swept his eyes across the endless horizon looking for any signs of trouble, knowing *Maggie* was like a red flag to a bull. Streicher finally broke the unbearable silence.

"We're heading south," he intoned over the intercom. "I think we can make it to the Adriatic Sea. We'll bail out, and, if we're lucky, we'll get picked up if our IFF (Identification Friend or Foe) is getting out." Joe shuttered in the confines of his cubbyhole. Bailing out over water was always dangerous. He would have to slip out of his harness some 50 feet over the water and free fall the rest of the way. Only in this way, he was always told, could he avoid getting tangled in his canopy and possibly drowning. The other small problem was that he couldn't swim a stroke. He felt a sickening lurch in his gut as he sat far removed from the rest of the crew.

Despite their hopeless situation, everybody still had a job to do. And they did it. While Streicher and Morrell struggled with the flight controls, Flight Engineer Clarence Jensen stood between them watching the gauges for any signs of trouble with the one good engine. John Reilly kept his post in the top turret, leaving only long enough to make sure the IFF radio signal was still working. Clark Fetterman and William Birchfield were busy trying to get a fix on their position, but it was impossible. Everything in the plane, including the navigation charts, were scattered all over the place from the turmoil of the dive out of formation. Like Joe, Ed O'Connor and Bill Kollar kept watch from the nose and waist windows.

Joe was still bedeviled by the whereabouts of the Junkers that had so quickly scurried away after the attack. He knew they would not give up so easily on such easy pickings. Maybe they were finishing off someone else first. Maybe they had to wait their turn, he thought.

"Suddenly, out of nowhere, one of 'em came screaming at us at 6 o'clock high," Joe remembers. *Maggie's Drawers* shuttered as the muffled chatter of the top guns rang out. It was John Reilly. But only one of his twin barrels was working, so he couldn't deliver the punch he needed.

"@#@# it all to hell," he cursed into his throat mike, as the fighter ducked down and kept closing in. It just wasn't Reilly's day. "I can't see him," he added. "He's all yours Joe."

"I see 'em," came the terse reply, as Joe turned his full attention to the job at hand. He knew he had to come up with something fast to outfox his tormentor. Remembering the time his bus driver had to be quick to keep his legs from being crushed in the accident outside Hartford, Joe came up with a plan. And, like the bus driver, success would depend entirely on flawless timing. He rode his guns in the stowed position, hoping his adversary would think he were hit. He waited a few seconds. He couldn't be sure, but it looked like the fighter was holding a steady course. It looked like the trap was working. Joe tightened his grip on his twin 50s until his fingers went numb. His hands began to sweat. His breath was fast and shallow. Only 600 yards now separated fighter and bomber. It was time. Joe yanked his guns up and squeezed the trigger, all in one motion. A hammering vibration echoed through his turret as he let go with two or three short bursts. Maybe four. He couldn't be sure in all the excitement.

"I nailed him," Joe barked through the roar of his guns as he watched a ribbon of bullets rip into the Junkers. He paused for a closer look. The fighter kept coming. "Damn," he screamed at the top of his lungs, sure that he had hosed the fighter from stem to stern. Then to his great relief, he saw the canopy of the two-seater slide open. He blinked in disbelief as he watched both crewmen struggle to their feet and hurl themselves out. In the next split second he knew why. The left wing of the Junkers sheared off. The fighter went into a spin.

"When I looked down I saw two parachutes," says Joe in a conciliatory tone. "I hoped they made it." As the mid-day twilight over Steyr slowly returned to a vista of majestic blue, the embattled 15th Air Force began to count its losses: 36 heavy bombers were gone, including three from the 98th. Eleven per cent of the mission and 360 men were missing, Joe Maloney among them. The Germans claimed the Allied losses were more like 54 Liberators and Flying Fortresses. By its own admission, the Luftwaffe lost 50 of its fighters. The Americans insisted it was closer to 115. Under a canopy of flak and fog, the Austrian factory town had fared somewhat better. The gothic houses and baroque churches of Steyr were spared as were its people, for the most part. Only 42 dead and 152 injured this time. Acceptable figures in light of the massive assault. The prime target, the Steyr-Daimler-Puch Waelzlogerwesr Ball bearing plant, was, however, a different story.

When the former arms factory was forced to close after the Great War, a decisive step was taken by Steyr in the direction of peacetime production. The plant would build automobiles instead. Steyr Daimler Puch AG was thus born. Making most of its own component parts, the fledgling company soon began to mass produce ball bearings in a building adjacent to the auto factory. By 1938, a much expanded Steyr-Daimler-Puch Waelzlogerwesr Company was a runaway success. When war broke out, it quickly became a strategic link in the vital German anti-friction bearings industry.

The demands of the war soon forced the company to expand again. Built in 1941, a new straight line production facility covered 500,000 square feet of floor space and housed 2,000 machine tools. By 1944 the labor force had grown to over 5,000. It was the largest manufacturer of bearings independent of the famous Schweinfurt complexes in neighboring Bavaria.

A thousand different types of ball, cylindrical and tapered roller bearings were soon coming off the production lines to feed the voracious appetite of the Nazi war machine. They were the lifeblood of its ships, planes, tanks and just about everything in between. After two failed attempts to

Heavy damage in Steyr, Austria.

flatten it in early 1944, the USAAF had understandably made the Steyr plant a top priority on April 2.

Despite its daunting losses, the 15th Air Force had delivered a decisive blow. Bombing was accurate and destruction extensive. Plant officials estimated damage at over 70 per cent. Of the 2,000 machines, 200 were totally destroyed, mainly in the grinding department and in the ball and roller works. Another five or six hundred were damaged but repairable. Half of the company's stock, four months of work, was pulverized.

No official count was ever recorded of the dead and wounded factory workers. Austrian records were notoriously inaccurate to keep Hitler's Third Reich from learning just how badly the war had been going. And, as always, civilians were forbidden from writing anything about the raid. Nevertheless, the deaths of two senior plant managers did survive official censorship.

When the air raid alarm sounded, book keeper Josef Fruhauf and security boss Heinrich Paternioner stepped outside the plant to see for themselves if the bombers were really coming. They were obliterated on the spot where they stood. Not a shred of them was ever found.

The altimeter on *Maggie's Drawers* now confirmed Fred Streicher's worst fears. One engine was not enough to keep the big bird flying much longer. They were steadily losing speed and altitude. The crew threw out everything that was not bolted down: flak jackets, helmets, ammunition and other heavy expendibles. It really didn't do any good but it gave the men some sense of hope. At least they were spared the ultimate horror in many situations like this. They didn't have to throw out the body of one of their dead buddies just to try to get back home.

Streicher turned off all non-essential systems to maximize power to the number three prop. Joe wondered if he had had a hand in making that engine back at the Pratt & Whitney plant in East Hartford. Probably not. But just maybe...

Only 45 minutes after they had been hit, *Maggie's Drawers* was down to 14,000 feet, a drop of 7,500 feet. But worse, airspeed was a miserly 130 mph, just above stall. Despite their best efforts, they knew the end was near. A cryptic order echoed through the ship's intercom.

"Prepare to bail out," entoned the voice of the co-pilot. "We'll abandon ship on my signal."

Snapping his cumbersome chest chute to the body harness he always wore, Joe lumbered towards the belly hatch. Looking down at his stuffed appearance, he gave the bundle a pat for good luck, thinking about the many times he had used it as a pillow on the long way back from a mission. Now it would have to save his life. Intercom chatter was kept to a minimum to clear the way for Morrell's bail-out signal. Then a stroke a luck.

"There's another Lib just ahead of us," came Streicher's reassuring voice. As tempting as it was for him to ask his new neighbor for help, the pilot maintained radio silence so as not to betray his position. It was the same with the other ship. The presence of a friendly face bolstered Joe's confidence. But the euphoria was short lived as 40-50 enemy fighters, mostly FW-190s, began slashing in and out of their uncertain path.

Better know as "Yellow Hornets" because of their distinctive canary yellow prop shafts, these enemy fighters were nothing to fool with. Equipped with a rugged air-cooled engine, they were heavily armored with solid steel on their shark like bellies. Every Allied airman knew the FW-190s were a bugger to take on. Sporting two heavy machine guns and four wing cannons, the 190s were the cock of the walk, especially when it came to a pair of beat up bombers. "They started circling the guy in front of us like a wagon train," says Joe. "I soon realized they were giving our guys time to bail out."

Sure enough, after 10 parachutes dotted the sky, the fighters moved in for target practice. The bomber went down in flames. On this day, at least, there was honor among enemies in the sky.

"Make ready to bail out," Streicher barked into the ship's intercom as Morrell punched the three bell bail-out warning.

"We're next," came the final warning from the cockpit. Joe was right. They did have to wait their turn. The tension inside the wretched ship was building, yet the indomitable spirit of the crew refused to give in. The airmen bristled at the very notion of giving up as the FW-190s closed in.

"I went back to my post just in case they decided to jump us," Joe says. "But they kept out of range of our guns going round and round in a big circle. We got the message." Always the gambler, Bill Kollar bet John Reilly that he could be the first one on the ground. His try was anything but pretty and darn near fatal. As he lunged headfirst through the waist window, he fetched up, his body halfway in and halfway out of the aircraft. The pressure of the slipstream pinned him so hard against the opening that he couldn't budge either way.

By now Joe had come forward, again satisfied there was nothing more he could do at his battle station. Trying hard to stifle a laugh at the near farcical scene that greeted him, Joe, and Art Fleming who had just crawled up from the ball, knew what they had to do. With a big yank, Kollar was back inside, blue lips and all. He grabbed a waist gun and started shooting. At first Joe thought he was just letting off steam. Then he saw a fighter going down off their left beam.

"That ain't one of ours," Kollar snorted. "Damn Krauts," he added as an afterthought. Without further ado, he let go of his gun grips, stepped forward, and, this time, dove straight through the belly hatch, followed quickly by Art Flemming who, likewise, disappeared in an instant. Towards the front of the ship, nose gunner Ed O'Connor, engineer Clarence

Jensen, bombardier Clark Fetterman and navigator William Birchfield were getting ready to jump through the nose-wheel hatch. However, they discovered to their horror that some rocket fragments had fused shut their escape route. They would have to find another way out.

Groping along on hands and knees, they began to look for an unobstructed path through the narrow passageway to the open bomb bay. It was their only hope, but the task was nearly impossible because the mid-section of the ship was littered with jagged pieces of twisted metal. Picking his way through the hellish maze, Fetterman had almost made it to the bomb bay when he ran into trouble. First, he felt his ripcord catch on something. Then, he heard a loud "pop". When the bombardier stood up, an expression of horror swept across his face. In his arms he held reams and reams of loose nylon. It was his parachute. He leaned over the bomb bay as if to exit, but was too terrified to jump. Not even his prized photo of Shirley Temple could help him now.

"I can't go! I can't!" he yelled in panic. "Jump," somebody ordered. "You've got to jump or you'll die! You have no choice."

John Reilly, who was still not having a good day, decided it was time for action. Sitting on the raised flight deck just behind Fetterman, he put both of his feet on the bombardier's back and literally kicked him out before he knew what hit him.

"As I held my breath and looked straight down through the bomb bay, I saw a glorious white dome," says Joe. Next through the gaping bomb bay went O'Connor, Jensen and Birchfield. Then Reilly. When his buddy's white canopy popped open, Joe smiled. Finally, Reilly was having a good day, everything considered. Just before he jumped, Reilly made sure the IFF knob on his radio was set to the "on" position that activated a locator beacon. There was a remote chance that another bomber in the area might pick up *Maggie's Drawers* last known position and report it to Allied Headquarters in Italy for what it was worth. Seven down. Three to go. The whole procedure had taken less than a minute. Joe pressed his throat mike for one last word to the cockpit.

"Back end clear. I'm going out. Good luck," were his only words.

"Thanks Joe," came Streicher's terse reply. "Get the hell out of here."

"See you on the ground, buddy," added Morrell warmly. "Don't get shot."

Removing his throat mike and headset, Joe sat down on the cold hard deck to collect his thoughts, conscious of only one thing, the mournful death rattle of engine number three. He had already decided he wouldn't be going through the bomb bay. It was too big and too intimidating.

Joe plunked his feet down through the small belly hatch behind the waist windows. The biting wind chilled him to the bone. Or was he just scared? He glanced at the hills and meadows rushing by below. Catching himself marveling at their beauty, he decided to check the snaps on his chute one more time just to make sure. When he saw that they were hooked securely to his body harness, he pulled in a deep breath. He wasn't going to do a regulation jump but at this point, he didn't care about rules and regulations. All he wanted was to get this thing over and done with.

A by-the-book bailout would have had him diving headfirst through the hatch. That was the only way, he was always instructed, that he could counteract the tremendous pressure of the slipstream. If he went feet first he ran a considerable risk of being slapped up against the underbelly of the ship. Or, if the wind caught his legs just so, he might slam his head against the edge of the hatch. Either way, it would not be a pretty sight. He was going to do it his way anyway.

Facing the tail end of the aircraft, Joe gritted his teeth, looked down again and fixed his stare on the rolling ground below. The good earth seemed closer now. He tried to swallow, but the dryness in his mouth wouldn't let him. He cinched the leg straps on his parachute harness a bit tighter. Either that, or risk a voice change when the chute snapped open. He was glad he remembered. Trying to stare down his fears, his thoughts turned to the people who had packed his chute. He prayed they had done a good job. He rolled his eyes again, this time at the thought of the times he used to use his pack as a cushion on the wet ground while waiting for a mission to begin.

Something out of the right waist window caught Joe's eye. It was a small city in the distant foothills. It looked so pretty, just sitting there in the bright sunlight. Suddenly he remembered the stories about Allied airmen being beaten to death by hostile civilians. He hoped there would be German soldiers down there instead to take him prisoner. Better that than facing an angry peasant with a pitch fork as far as he was concerned.

It was now or never. With a determined push of his trembling hands against the rugged cold steel, he pitched forward and spilled through the narrow hatch in one smooth motion. The speed of his exit surprised him. The 130 mile per hour blast of freezing air tore at his face and flimsy flying suit.

Disoriented, he had the sensation of floating for a moment, not falling. It was as though he were suspended in mid air. But the panic quickly passed as it dawned on him that he was actually outside of the airplane and still alive. So far so good. He had a short talk with God about making it the rest of the way. Clutching the D-ring, Joe paused before pulling the ripcord. He wanted to make sure he was clear of the prop-wash. He began to drift in and out of a kaleidoscope of childhood memories. He wanted to sleep. He knew he was going into shock. He tried to concentrate, but everything seemed to be in slow motion. Fighting to control his runaway emotions, he squeezed the D-ring with all his might and gave it a hard yank. The chute cracked open. The white nylon billowed above him. His "cushion" was okay. He felt like his groin had jumped into his throat as he fetched up hard. Other airmen had warned him the sudden jerk of the canopy would be enough to rip his shoes off.

His 24 foot chute was too small for a man of his size. The pilots had 28 foot seat chutes which made a big difference in their rate of descent. Joe now worried about breaking his ankles when it came time to land. He said another quick prayer.

Back in the cockpit, Streicher and Morrell were struggling to stabilize *Maggie's Drawers* long enough for them to scramble out. As busy as he

Novo Mesto. Joe and his crew ended up on the ground only a few miles from this heavily German occupied town in Slovenija in 1944.

was, Streicher had also noticed the same city Joe had spotted earlier. It was Novo Mesto in Slovenija, a city in northern Yugoslavia heavily occupied by the Germans. Neither one had any way of knowing this since a fix on their last position was never made. With the aircraft finally trimmed and on auto-pilot, Streicher and Morrell clambered out of the ravaged flight deck and onto the deserted bomb bay below. They were shocked by the extent of damage that greeted them. It was time to get out of there.

The co-pilot jumped. When it came Streicher's turn, he hesitated. He realized he had forgotten his cigarettes. That simply wouldn't do. He might need them for barter with some local peasant. Besides, he reasoned, this was no time to try to quit smoking. Losing precious time, he picked his way back to the cockpit to retrieve his smokes, retraced his steps to the bomb bay and dove out. *Maggie's Drawers* was now on her own. But only for a moment. The enemy fighters quickly moved in for the kill, as 10 frightened men tumbled towards a hostile, unknown land.

The cacophony of howling engines, flak bursts and machine gunfire that had filled his world just moments before fell silent as Joe floated serenely towards earth's hushed embrace. The air he drew into his lungs now smelled of spring. It felt cool and inviting after sucking back oxygen from a smelly rubber mask for so long. He at least felt good just to be breathing normally again.

The silence that greeted him was eerie. He felt alone. He cursed the fact that he probably wouldn't even see his 21st birthday in just two days time. He felt even more alone. Conscious of the swarm of fighters still circling the jump area, Joe didn't know which would be worse, getting shot while hanging like a sack of potatoes in his harness, or having his chute spilled by the prop-wash of a fighter and free falling the rest of the way. Despite his gruesome fears, he held onto one last hope.

When he had first joined the 98th, he ran into a number of airmen who had survived a grand, but failed, Allied attempt to shorten the war by six months. An unorthodox low-level bombing raid was carried out against Hitler's vital oil refineries at Ploesti, Romania on August 1, 1943. However, waiting for them was German General Alfred Gerstenberg, an air defense genius, who had spent three years building the heaviest antiaircraft system for a single target in the world. The American losses were staggering. Out of 164 B-24s, 53 were shot down, a gruesome loss of 30 percent.

The few lucky ones to come back alive were nervous wrecks, as Joe recalled. But what he remembered most about these battle hardened veterans was their advice to the new airmen. They pleaded with the fighter pilots and air gunners not to shoot any Germans in their parachutes. As he hung in mid-air, Joe could only hope that he might somehow reap the benefit of this sound advice.

One of the fighter pilots buzzed Joe, probably with the intention of checking him out for a side arm. The Luftwaffe still had a reputation for shooting armed airmen, parachute or not. Lucky for Joe, he had decided to leave his pistol home that day. What good were six measly shots anyway, he reasoned.

The German pilot smiled and waved as he closed to within 300 feet. Joe was shocked to see how young he was. He looked like a fresh faced kid hardly out of high school. At this stage of the game in the German air war, he probably was. Joe was too preoccupied to wave back. Too scared too, although he appreciated the unusual gesture.

Squinting into the bright midday sun, 11-year-old Anton Kos knew that something wasn't quite right. While gathering brush along a wooded footpath to help his family decorate for Easter, the young lad was suddenly distracted by an unusual noise. He could still hear the church bells ringing in his village of Doljni Mahasoveck, near the rugged Croatian border of southern Slovenija. But it was something else, something odd sounding, that drew his eyes upwards. He fixed his gaze in the direction of the advancing sound. Something caught his eye. It was bright and silvery, like a huge metal bird. He cupped his hands over his eyes for a better look. There, in the distance, was a huge four engine plane. Anton blinked. The plane got bigger. It was flying low. Too low, he thought. And there was something wrong with the engines. They didn't sound right. He also noticed a long trail of white mist coming out of the right wing. He watched in awe as the huge ship made a long, almost graceful U-turn and disappeared from sight. A column of black smoke rose up in the distance. The boy took off on a dead run to have a look, a little bit scared about what he was sure to find.

Just down the road, in the hamlet of Vinja Vas, Jost Rolc had been watching the same thing. Earlier in the day, the 16 year old had cheered when he saw the high flying bombers making their way north to Austria. The armadas always meant hope for him, hope that someday soon the war would be over.

Jost had heard about the Americans and their big planes. It was the talk of his village every time a formation went over. But now he noticed one of the planes was flying very low and by itself. He also saw two German Messerschmitts closing in on the bomber with machine guns blazing at full bore. Then, something odd happened. Jost watched in disbelief as one of the pilots made mincemeat out of a couple of sheep grazing in a nearby field, the result of over shooting his target. He found the whole scene almost comical in spite of the dire circumstances. In the next instant, Jost watched as the bomber made a long sweeping U-turn to the left, teetered momentarily as it stalled out, and took a steep nose dive.

At the end of its torturous descent, the stricken B-24 slammed into the ground with an explosive rain of tangled metal and a searing blast of spewing gasoline. A mushroom of billowing black smoke marked her grave.

Maggie's Drawers, that had so faithfully seen her crew through so many grueling missions, was reduced to a pyre of twisted, smoking wreckage. It was the final flight of *Maggie's Drawers*.

Joe felt a sudden change in temperature as the ground leapt up at him. The warm air soothed his cold, aching body. He was drifting towards a farmhouse perched on a knoll at the end of a long valley. It was the only sign of civilization he could make out. He didn't know if that was a good sign or not. He desperately scanned the empty sky one last time for any sign of his buddies. Nothing. He hadn't caught as much as a glimpse of them in the long 15 minutes since leaving the aircraft. The ground was coming up faster now. He pulled hard on one of the risers to spill some of the air from his chute, hoping he could slip sideways far enough to avoid mashing his legs on the farmhouse roof. He worried about spilling too much air and collapsing the whole darn thing.

"I cleared the roof all right, but I landed so hard on a rocky pasture that my head went flying right past my knees right into the ground," he recalls.

Everything went blank. Coming to a minute or so later, he had a terrific pain in his forehead. Reaching up, he felt a deep gash over his left eye. Gingerly he struggled to his feet, wiping as much blood as he could from his throbbing head. He suddenly came face to face with a young peasant women. He didn't know who was more terrified at that moment.

Still dazed, so he couldn't be sure, but it looked to him that the young woman was holding her arms up in the air. Joe was confused. Surely she wasn't trying to surrender to him, he tried to reason. As his woolly eyesight began to focus, he realized to his horror that something entirely different was happening.

The woman had her arms up in the air all right. But she wasn't about to surrender. And by the looks on her face she wasn't from the welcoming committee of the local Chamber of Commerce either. Joe was staring at the business end of a very pointy pitch fork. His worst nightmare had just come true.

CHAPTER EIGHT

On The Run

If human beings are really determined to do something, they will do it, even if all calculation shows it to be impossible.
Tito
April 1943

On April 6, 1941, German ground troops, with the help of Italy, Hungary and Bulgaria, stormed into Yugoslavia after Belgrade collapsed under a crush of Luftwaffe bombers. It was punishment for Yugoslavia's refusal to permit German supplies and troops bound for Turkey, use of its railways. The Axis campaign was short and decisive. Internal political dissension had already left the Balkans with virtually no chance of resisting the Wehrmacht steamroller. Victory for the invaders was therefore only a matter of time.

Eleven days later, the High Command of the Yugoslav Army capitulated. The Kingdom of Yugoslavia had come apart in less than two weeks. The Royal Family, including 17 year old King Peter, along with the entire government, fled to Britain where they set up a government in exile. Out of this crisis arose the war cry of labor organizer, come revolutionary, Josip Broz-code name Tito.

Within months of the Axis occupation, Tito began to organize guerrilla bands of men and women armed with nothing more than cudgels, axes and old sporting rifles. But, they were a people's army, hell-bent on driving out the fascist invaders. They were Partisans with no ties to the exiled government. Tito was a communist who proudly wore the red star on his cap.

The Partisans quickly developed a broad base of operations, soon establishing governments in areas they controlled. This was especially true after 1943. Almost solely supported by the Soviets at first, Tito's Partisans eventually won recognition from the other Allies. With additional war materiel at their disposal, they soon replaced their old nemesis, the royalist Chetniks under General Draza Mihajlovic, as the foremost resistance force in occupied Yugoslavia.

The Partisans' increasing power was also facilitated in part by their control of considerable territory and arms during the time the Italian forces surrendered to the Allies. Although the civil war between the Partisans and the Chetniks would continue to play itself out with vicious fighting between them until the Germans surrendered in 1945, the Partisans now clearly had the upper hand.

Tito commanded 200,000 troops divided into eight corps and 26 divisions. He controlled one third of Yugoslavia by 1944, mostly small towns, villages and the hills. Predictably, Germany responded in kind. It threw 14 divisions, two SS regiments and five divisions of non-Germans under the aegis of the Nazis into the Balkans. For the most part, their 300,000 heavily armed soldiers controlled the population centers, the larger cities and towns, where they did not have to spread themselves over such large distances.

For Allied bomber crews, the proximate resources and fighting ability of the Partisans and the Germans were significant factors when it came to their chances of survival. Whenever a crew bailed out, each side made a mad dash to get to the downed airmen first. This was the harsh political landscape of Yugoslavia that greeted Joe and his crew on the afternoon of April 2, 1944.

On that same afternoon, a Partisan intelligence officer by the name of Stanislav Erjavec knew he would have to give the Germans a run for their money. Attached to the 1,000 strong Cankarjeva Brigada in southeastern Slovenija, the 19 year old freedom fighter was in a dense forest stand just outside the village of Pristava, beneath the magnificent rolling hills of Gorjanci. He was on an urgent mission, trying to get a message from Brigade Headquarters in Podgrad to the Fourth Battalion at Mrasevo, about a half day's trek away. Stopping to figure out his fastest route, he could hear the chatter of machine guns and the occasional rumble of a howitzer off in the distance. Suddenly, a piercing thunder drew Stanislav's eyes skyward.

At first he noticed 10 tiny dots way up in the sky. It took him a split second to realize they were parachutes. He knew they had to be Americans. He had often seen their huge armadas passing overhead. Wetting a finger, Stanislav checked the wind. His heart sank. It was blowing west northwest towards Novo Mesto. The tiny white dots were drifting right into enemy hands! "Then I saw a huge four engine plane come into view," he remembers. "It couldn't have been more than a few hundred feet off the ground."

The hills of Gorjanci, where he stood, were very strategic. They were the buffer between two very different territories, Dolenjeko and Bela Krajina. Dolenjeko was the stronghold of the Germans and the Bela Garda. The Bela Garda, better known as the White Guard, was an anti-Communist group of locals who collaborated with the Nazis with the full blessing and support of the established religion in the region, the Roman Catholic Church. The White Guard was no different than other anti-Bolshevik armies in Eastern Europe which took up arms after 1941, and especially after 1943 and 1944, in their struggle against emerging communism. Unlike their German brethren, they dressed like civilians, making it impossible for anyone to distinguish them as the enemy. In fact, there were often divided loyalties within the same families, some siding with the Partisans while others worked for the White Guard. Brother often killed brother when the two sides met. The White Guard's reputation for ruthlessness did, however, set them apart. Joe had heard some pretty awful stories about the collaborators, but one tale in particular made his blood run cold because it involved a bomber crew.

After the crew bailed out and was captured by the White Guard, the officers were strung up with meat hooks inserted through their lower jaws into the roof of their mouths. They were left to dangle, twist, gurgle and drown in their own blood. The enlisted men were not harmed. But they were forced to watch, then given their officers' dog tags and told to return with their story of what would happen to other crews if they fell into the wrong hands. Joe had made up his mind that he would rather face an angry civilian or a German soldier any day than take his chances with those bastards.

Particularly menacing within the occupied region of Dolenjeko was Novo Mesto, the medieval city founded by Rudolf 1V of Habsburg in 1365. This once splendid town had been a mecca for the arts, literature and other Eastern Europe culture through the centuries. By 1944 Novo Mesto was little more than an ugly fortress, caged in by razor sharp barbed wire and heavily fortified bunkers. First occupied by the Italians after the Axis crushed Yugoslavia, the Germans now boasted a formidable presence with its 14th SS Panzer Regiment, the 13th Armored Tank and Artillery Division along with a huge communications platoon.

With over 700 well equipped Nazi troops and more than a thousand White Guard soldiers at its disposal, Novo Mesto was armed to the teeth. In addition, 10 airplanes were at the enemy's ready on an airfield at nearby Cerklje.

On the other side of Gorjanci, to the southwest of Novo Mesto, Bela Krajina was liberated territory under Partisan control. The fate of Joe and his crew lay squarely on which side of the Gorjanci hills they would be lucky, or unlucky, enough to come down on.

As the tiny puff balls slowly mushroomed into fluttering domes of white nylon, a smile came across Stanislov Erjavec's face. Mother Nature had a change of heart.

"The wind shifted at the last minute and started to blow the chutes towards me," he says. "All of them came down between the villages of Jurna vas and Orehek, inside Bela Krajina."

The airmen were on the right side of the mountain, in free territory. They were safe, but only for the moment. The Germans in Novo Mesto, already alerted by their fighter pilots, were quick off the mark. They sent out three patrols to root out the airmen, no matter where they were, with standing orders to kill anyone who tried to get in their way.

Stanislov took off on a run. He knew he didn't have much time. He knew he had to get to the airmen first. By now the rat-tat-tat of enemy machine guns was getting louder. The Germans were already fighting their way through a Partisan patrol to get to their booty, the American airmen.

"After running across some open fields as fast as I could, I spotted a man standing in the open about a hundred meters in front of me," he recalls. "He already had his parachute off. When he saw me he turned to run in the opposite direction towards the Germans. I yelled "Stoj"" (stop).

The airman turned towards his pursuer and raised his arms in surrender. He looked piqued and frightened, all at the same time. But, most of all, he looked bewildered. Stanislav had seen the look before on the faces of other airmen in similar circumstances. He knew the look of shock and despair. He also knew he had to try to calm the man down.

Punctuating his words with frantic hand gestures, Stanislav tried desperately to make the airman understand that he was only trying to help him. He pointed to his blue felt cap with the red star on the peak and said "Partisan" over and over again. He also gestured towards the woods behind the flyer with the words "Germanski, Germanski." The airman still didn't get it. Stanislav thought he would try one more thing.

"I leaned over and picked up his leather flying helmet and gently put it back on his head. He finally got the message that I was the good guy."

After a quick bear hug, they made a hasty retreat to the nearby village of Pristava, dodging a couple of enemy patrols along the way. Stanislav turned his young charge over to another group of Partisans for safe keeping. He had much work to do. He was not only a courier but also an informer for the Partisans, trusted by the Germans. He often went to Novo Mesto to see what the enemy was up to, especially their troop strength and deployment. At the moment, though, he had to get his important message through to the Fourth Battalion at Mrasevo. He was sure his superiors would understand the reasons for his delay. He never saw the young flyer again. (Joe is convinced it was Bill Kollar).

On the side of a steep wooded slope, the Partisan squadron commander of the 5th Slovene Brigade was in the midst of a pitched battle with the 14th SS Panzer Regiment pushing in from Novo Mesto. Franc Planic was a wiry 21-year-old in charge of 160 tough-as-nails men and women of the 3rd Battalion. Looking up from the fray, he too had seen the crippled bomber and the parachutes.

Charging down a hill in the direction of the tumbling parachutes, Planic came to a rocky creek. Leaning over to catch his breath for a moment, he looked up, only to see a young man struggling out of his parachute harness. Only the spring swollen brook separated them. Undaunted, the squadron commander leapt across, leaving the flyer more confused than startled.

Within a few minutes, the two men were joined by another Partisan, Marica Lakovic. It made for an interesting three way conversation, considering the language problem. The USAC had obviously done a poor job of briefing Joe's crew on just who their allies were.

"The airman was making some kind of sign language and so were we," says Franc Planic. "But I guess the whole thing looked pretty ridiculous because pretty soon we all started to laugh. Everything was okay after that. He knew we were there to help him."

With the American in tow, Planic and Lakovic made their way to Battalion Headquarters in Lakunice, several miles away, where three other members of Joe's crew were already waiting. Things were beginning to look up.

A woman by the name of Franciska Sparovec had played a key role in saving these three other men. After they had wandered into her village of Gornja Tezka Voda, she insisted they stay put and rest. Sitting on a long wooden bench in front of her modest home, they were offered goulash. But all they really wanted was her wine and brandy. They were far too excited to eat anything but they did manage to gulp down some hefty doses of her homemade brew. This delay probably saved their lives because the entire area was soon ringed with enemy soldiers.

Unknown to the small band of flyers was the fact that Franciska's home was the regional headquarters for the resistance movement. She managed to waylay her unsuspecting guests long enough for several Partisans to reach her house. That evening the trio was taken a short distance to Lakunice. The next day the three airmen, along with the man who Franc Planic had saved, were escorted to Podgrad, a large Partisan center.

With skill and daring, other Partisans, like Milan Zagorc, a 22-year-old commander of the 1st Battalion, also helped snatch several other crewmen from the enemy's jaws. A clutch of German tanks had been closing in on three of the airmen hiding under a big fir tree in a farmer's field. But Milan

Zagorc managed to get to them first, albeit, by only seconds. After hustling them off to Podgrad the next day, Zagorc and his small band of battled hardened men returned to meet more Germans sweeping in from Novo Mesto. Like his comrades, he never asked the names of the men he helped save that day.

Art Fleming was in a real pickle when he came down. Dangling in a tree after the ropes to his chute got snagged, a Partisan came along and cut him down. There was no mistaking this gesture. Out of appreciation, Art offered Joze Sladek the only thing he really prized among his pitiful possessions, a pack of cigarettes. Joze was delighted. They began their overnight trek to Podgrad at dusk.

Fred Streicher wasn't as lucky. Losing valuable time in getting out of the aircraft because of his cigarettes – he was cursing himself for that by now – he was hopelessly separated from the rest of the crew. To make matters worse, he had landed with such a shattering thump that he sprained both ankles.

Fortunately for Streicher, Franc Brulc and his group of Partisans happened to be in the right place at the right time. They saw the pilot's plight unfold from their wooded hideout, a short distance away. Trying to regroup his men after forcing a German patrol into retreat, Brulc dropped everything to rush over to the crippled airman with his rifle at the ready.

"I was hoping he was a German because he had such a fine watch, which I fully intended to be mine," he recalls with a smile. "He was swearing up quite storm in German, but his uniform was American. I couldn't figure out who's side he was on."

Streicher only made matters worse by continuing to curse in a loud voice in German, a habit he had picked up as a child whenever he lost his temper. He had stored up quite a few choice words from his German born parents. It would have been his undoing had it not been for the tremendous patience and good judgment of his would be captors. Partisans seldom, if ever, took prisoners. Dead men didn't need guards. Figuring he had to be an American because of his uniform, not to mention his demeanor, Brulc decided that Streicher could keep his watch. There was no time for small talk as the Partisans grabbed the injured pilot by the belt and heaved him up on a horse. His parachute was draped over him for warmth. It was two days before Streicher saw Podgrad and the rest of his crew. Franc Brulc didn't make the trip. He figured the bomber would be more interesting. He had never seen one of them up close. Dodging around enemy patrols, he made it to the crash site in no time. He was shocked by the amount of devastation that greeted him.

"There were fires all over the place from spilled fuel and flying debris," he remembers. " A farmhouse and a Kozolec (hayrack) were burning, but the plane itself was still in one piece." *Maggie's Drawers* had bored a six foot deep trench into a farmer's field high on a bluff overlooking the tiny village of Tolsti vrh. Inside liberated territory, the crash site was a mere eight miles from Novo Mesto. Miraculously, the bomber had narrowly missed the castle "Gracarjev turn", built as a fortress to close the narrow passage of lands to Novo Mesto against invaders in another time, the Turks and Serbs in 1328. In 1944 Gracarjev turn was occupied by the Schoppel family, friends of the Partisans. Just down the road, Tolsti vrh itself was a hotbed of White Guard. In this region, enemies were practically neighbors.

Young Anton Kos had also made it to the crash site. He couldn't get over how one of the plane's engines was completely torn off and buried deep in the ground from the impact. He peeked inside the blackened, yawning guts of the broken ship. The fuselage was buckled and heaved. Twisted pieces of metal, gun parts and broken instruments, with not as much as a shard of glass left, were scattered all over the place. Ammunition belts were still slung from the bulkheads. Loose cartridges were strewn everywhere. The top bulkhead was partially collapsed. The waist windows were twisted and bent, almost beyond recognition. A heavy stench of oil and fuel choked the air.

A group of villagers talked excitedly among themselves, pointing at a long cylindrical object on the ground that looked like a bomb. They had no way of knowing it was only a charred and harmless spent oxygen tank.

Stepping back into the glare of the afternoon sun, Anton Kos had had enough. The thought of spotting a body in all that blackness sent shivers down his spine. Surely, he reasoned, not everyone could have made it out there alive. Nudging himself deeper into the collective security of the gathering crowd, he too had eyed the long metal object on the ground. He didn't know what to make of it either.

Everything of any use on the B-24 was used in Partisan workshops for the needs of the army.

Anton decided it was time to go. The White Guard was close by and that always spelled trouble. Although this was Partisan territory, the enemy could, and often did, interdict anywhere and anytime with deadly force. One hundred and thirty Partisans had already been betrayed and slaughtered by the local German sympathizers in Tolsti vrh only a few months earlier. Tricked into going inside a barn on the pretext of a meeting, they perished when the doors were barricaded from the outside and the place was burned to the ground. With the atrocity still fresh on their minds, the crowd began to thin out and was soon gone. They knew from experience that this was not the time or place to press their luck.

The Germans had already expelled all the intelligentsia, and some 10,000 peasant farmers from Slovenija. They had banned the Slovene language in public, destroyed Slovene books and jailed or executed those who resisted. As cold blooded as the Germans were, it was the murderous White Guard whom the Partisans and their supporters feared the most. So hated were the collaborators, that when the British returned over 10,000 of them to their homeland from Austria, where they had fled at the end of the war, special divisions of the Yugoslav Army executed them without trial. A two front war always came at a high price.

In the weeks to follow, an army of heavily armed scavengers descended on *Maggie's Drawers*, for she was a source rich in the many things the Partisans desperately needed. Machine guns and radio transmitters were especially prized. Aluminum from the fuselage was melted down and turned into forks, knives, spoons, plates, and other utensils in underground workshops scattered throughout the hills.

Civilians were allowed to pick through the wreckage only after the Partisans were satisfied they had salvaged everything they could for the war effort. The peasants especially prized pieces of the fuselage that they could turn into doors or walls for their chicken coops. Anything with "Made in U.S.A." stamped on it was always fought over. *Maggie's Drawers* now truly belonged to Slovenija.

Months later, Anton Kos and some of his friends went back to the crash site with a horse and cart to retrieve the half buried motor. By that time the White Guard had been pushed well back from the territory and it was safe. "The man who owned the land said it would be all right as long as we filled in the hole," he recalls with a grin. "I sold the engine to a junk dealer for some pocket change, but I kept a few small pieces as souvenirs."

Joe Maloney was a very worried man. The young woman with the pitchfork still hadn't said a word. She just stood there stone faced. He couldn't tell whether she were friend or foe, but, somehow, he really didn't want to push the issue. He had heard too many stories about these people, stories of how rural folk in occupied countries seldom took kindly to downed airmen out of fear of retribution from the Germans.

A treasured piece of any airman's parachute was always the nylon which Partisan women turned into blouses and even wedding dresses.

Joe had often been warned that some peasants would think nothing of plunging a pitchfork into an airman and tossing his body into a dung pile to rot. When some of these unfortunate victims were later recovered by the Allies, their bodies were peppered with small round holes-all perfectly spaced. Joe shuttered at the thought. However, fate was on his side that day. The girl's father happened to be away that afternoon. He would be among the 10,000 White Guard to be liquidated after the war.

Joe slowly unbuckled his parachute harness. It had occurred to him that the young lady might be more interested in the parachute" than in him. He had heard stories about how the peasants in Yugoslavia treasured the silk, and later nylon material, for making blouses, underwear and even wedding dresses. The more he thought about it, the more it made sense to him. After all, the locals had to be hard up for just about everything. He decided to make his move.

"I pointed to her and then to my parachute several times," he recalls, "trying to get her to pick the thing up."

At first she stood her ground, not budging an inch. But, then, the young woman shifted her granite like stare to the bundle of nylon heaped up between them. Joe's hunch was right! He knew, it was now or never.

"As soon as she stooped over to gather it up, I took off like a shot. I never looked back, but I bet she was just as relieved as I was."

They had not exchanged as much as a single word during the whole encounter. Joe didn't really care. All he wanted was to get away from there as fast as he could.

Running into the woods, he stood in the shadows of some tall pine trees and stared out into an open field in front of him. Whipping across the sloping meadow, he had almost reached the safety of a thicket when he was

102

confronted again. This time a young lad no more than 10 years old was blocking his path. "Americanski, Americanski," the boy kept repeating.

"He knew where I had come from." Joe says. "When I pointed to the sky he nodded. I figured he had seen my parachute."

The lad handed Joe a flask of wine which he promptly downed in a couple of swigs. He couldn't believe how raw his throat was. His panic was worse than he thought. Thrusting the empty container back into the boy's small hands, Joe offered an abrupt nod of thanks and took off in full flight again.

"As I ran along the edge of the meadow looking for a good spot to duck into the woods, I heard someone shout "Tito-Americanski" from somewhere behind me," remembers Joe. "My blood ran cold. I knew it wasn't the boy this time." It was the deep voice of a grown man. Everybody and his dog must have seen him coming, he fretted. Slowly turning around, he spotted two men coming towards him. They had machine guns. Unarmed and exhausted, Joe could neither fight nor flee. He just stood there.

When they caught up to him, the two men kept repeating "Tito-Americanski" while moving their index fingers together. They were trying to tell the frightened airman that Tito and Americans were on the same side. But, like the rest of his crew, Joe just didn't get it.

The men in the rag-tag uniforms started walking towards the woods and motioned for Joe to follow them. Figuring he was about to take a bullet in the head, he made a mad dash for it. At least he wouldn't have to die at the sharp end of some pitchfork, he mused.

"When they caught up with me they grabbed me and pushed me to the ground," Joe recalls. "They didn't beat me but their eyes told me they meant business."

With Joe in the middle, the two men started to walk in single file through the thick forest. They trudged on for what seemed like hours, not stopping once. Not a word was spoken. Joe was getting so exhausted, to the point of giddiness, that he no longer cared what the two strangers had in store for him.

Breaking into a clearing on the brow of a tree lined hill late in the afternoon, a small village came into view. In the distance, Joe could make out a church steeple and smoke curling from the chimneys of some quaint looking houses. He was struck by the beauty of the place, in spite of his situation. In another 15 minutes, he found himself in the middle of the village. Word of the stranger soon spread from house to house, and, before long, a crowd started dropping by for a closer look at this big six foot, 200 pound man from the heavens. He was quite a sight, with his handsome blue flight suit and all.

"One of the men came up to me and gave me a big bearhug," says Joe. "I was getting the feeling I was among friends, but I still couldn't be sure because nobody spoke English." It was all quite maddening, not knowing what was going on. Finally, evening fell. Time to eat.

A group of peasants beckoned Joe to join them around a large open fire. He accepted. He hadn't eaten since well before dawn and then it had only been toast and coffee. Could this possibly be the same day, he wondered? His meager breakfast in Lecce that morning seemed so long ago and far away.

"Polenta, polenta," a bedraggled looking man exclaimed as he ladled up a bowl of something thick and hot from a large communal pot and handed it to Joe.

The church and rectory next door in Podgrad where Joe spent his first night after his rescue by the Partisans.

"I thought he was saying "plenty," as in "plenty to eat," but after I took my first spoonful, I realized he meant it was corn meal mush," he says. "I should have known that because I used to eat the stuff all the time back home."

Suppressing a gnawing anxiety over exactly who these people were, Joe greedily devoured the offering. It didn't taste like much, but it filled his empty stomach. Each mouthful went down like sandpaper. His throat was still on fire. Ignoring the inquisitive stares of his hosts, Joe continued to shove the food down his throat, no matter how much it hurt. It was then that he began to realize no one was actually standing watch over him. There were no guards around as far as he could tell. He no longer felt like a prisoner. No matter. Escape was the farthest thing from his mind anyway.

The fate of his crewmates weighed heavily on Joe's mind as he curled up with a heavy wool blanket on the rough-hewn floor of the village rectory. At least he was in a good place to pray. And pray he did. From the look of the rectory and the church next door, he surmised the villagers were Roman Catholics. That suited him just fine. As lonely and frightened as he was, at least something was familiar.

Despite his exhaustion, sleep would not come. For the first time in his life, Joe felt completely abandoned. Everything seemed so hopeless. War was hell all right, but in a way he never expected.

The next morning dawned bright and sunny. Just being alive bright-
ened Joe's spirits. An elderly couple greeted him with warm smiles and an
invitation to breakfast in their home next door, if he had read their signals
right. He had, and was soon sitting down to a frugal meal of bread and milk
at a crude but clean table. He could tell they didn't have much. The place
was small, its contents sparse. The floor was made of rough planks. Robust
with the ruddy complexions of hard working peasant folk, the old man and
woman seemed pleased to be sharing what little they had. Joe tried his best
to force a smile of gratitude. He had already decided to give up any feeble
attempts at conversation.

As he was about to take his last mouthful, Joe heard a loud commotion
coming from somewhere outside. Men and women, speaking in hurried,
excited tones, were racing by the window towards the center of the village.
Joe stepped outside for a look see. There, sauntering up the narrow dirt
road was the prettiest sight he had ever seen. Looking like he didn't have a
care in the world was none other than Bill Kollar.

"How the hell are ya Bill," Joe yelled.

Completely caught by surprise, Kollar looked up, and, for a split second, he couldn't believe his eyes.

"Joe!" he hollered. "What ya doin here?"

"Same as you, I guess," came the happy reply. "Captured, or saved.
Whatever. Good to see you 'ol buddy."

At last, Joe had someone to talk to. After the excitement of their reunion, they got down to some serious talk about the rest of the crew. It was
now almost 24 hours since they had all bailed out. Joe wasn't exactly
alarmed, but he was very concerned about the others. Maybe, just maybe,
he and Kollar were the only ones who survived.

"They all jumped," Joe reassured his friend. "I was the last one out
except for Fred and George up front. I know they had to make it."

Kollar could add nothing to ease Joe's mind. The hours lingered. Then,
three men appeared at the edge of the village. They didn't look like they
were locals, but Joe couldn't be sure at first glance. When they got a bit
closer, he realized to his great relief that he was staring into the faces of
John Reilly, Clarence Jensen and Clark Fetterman. Keeping the trio company was a small band of men wearing a red star on their caps.

Several hours later, three more crewmen turned up, again with an escort, William Birchfield, Art Flemming and the new guy, Ed O'Connor.
They were pretty unscathed considering their ordeal. Birchfield had a nasty
bump on his head as a result of an argument with a rock when he landed.
Other than that (by now Joe's gash was healing nicely) they were all okay.
Eight out of 10. Only the pilot and co-pilot were still missing out there
somewhere.

First light the following morning brought in one more straggler. It was

George Morrell. Perhaps because of his boyish looks, or maybe because he was so new to the crew, Joe felt sorry for him. Throwing his arms around his co-pilot, Joe offered his reassurance. Morrell had tears in his eyes, tears of joy from knowing that he might get out of this mess alive.

That left only Fred Streicher among the missing. But not for long. At around noontime, he galloped triumphantly into town. With his parachute fluttering in the wind he looked like some caped crusader about to save the day. That was Fred Streicher. Always the ham. The crew let out a collective sigh. They couldn't believe their good luck. For Joe, it was an extra special day. It was his birthday. He had actually lived to see 21 in spite of his dire predictions.

Soon the airmen had some answers to their most vexing questions. A man by the name of Trileajev-Janez Ambrozic, a Partisan leader who had lived and worked in the United States before the war, came to the village to fill them in. He spoke in a heavy accent but the meaning of his words was clear. They had landed very close to the German lines, he told them, but they were safe.

"Janez told us about Marshall Tito," says Joe. "He explained that the Partisans would risk their lives to save us but in return we were never to ask the name of anyone who helped us or where we had been."

The reason was obvious. If an airman were captured, he would be tortured until he revealed all. The Partisan escape routes would therefore be jeopardized for other airmen who were sure to follow. Joe didn't know that he was in a village called Podgrad, one of Tito's enclaves, only six miles from Novo Mesto.

From other bits of information they could glean from the man with the funny accent, the airmen learned that they would soon be taken away to a Partisan controlled airstrip. From there, they would be flown back to Italy. The plan sounded simple enough to Joe and the others. But would it work?

Just where this airfield was, or how long it would take to get there, they were not told. Neither were they given any hint about when the escape attempt might begin. The Partisans operated on a "need to know" basis. The airmen had little choice but to cool their heels until they were told otherwise by these strangers.

The 700 year old hamlet of Podgrad stood on a knoll among the sweeping valleys and majestic mountains of southeastern Slovenija. Its two dozen houses and 80 residents lived in the shadow of an imposing stone church perched high on a hill at the edge of the village. The church, and the rectory next door, served as divisional headquarters for the Partisans. At the end of the flagstone path leading from the church, stood a communal well. After drawing their daily drinking water, the peasants would set out each morning to eke out an existence from the rough, yet fertile land.

From the rectory headquarters, the Cankarjeva Brigada sent out an ur-

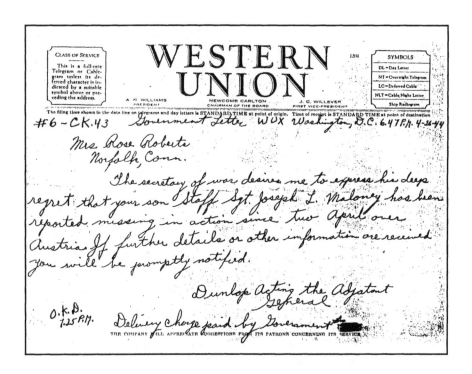

CLASS OF SERVICE

This is a full-rate Telegram or Cablegram unless its deferred character is indicated by a suitable symbol above or preceding the address.

WESTERN UNION

A. N. WILLIAMS
PRESIDENT

NEWCOMB CARLTON
CHAIRMAN OF THE BOARD

J. C. WILLEVER
FIRST VICE-PRESIDENT

SYMBOLS

DL = Day Letter
NT = Overnight Telegram
LC = Deferred Cable
NLT = Cable Night Letter
Ship Radiogram

The filing time shown in the date line on telegrams and day letters is STANDARD TIME at point of origin. Time of receipt is STANDARD TIME at point of destination

#6 - CK.43   Government Letter   WUX   Washington, D.C. 6.47P.M. 4-24-44

Mrs. Rose Roberts
Norfolk, Conn.

The secretary of war desires me to express his deep regret that your son Staff Sgt. Joseph L. Maloney has been reported missing in action since two April over Austria. If further details or other information are received you will be promptly notified.

Dunlop Acting the Adjutant General

O.K.D.
7.25 P.M.

Delivery Charge paid by Government

THE COMPANY WILL APPRECIATE SUGGESTIONS FROM ITS PATRONS CONCERNING ITS SERVICE

gent radio message to the Allies that Fred Streicher's crew was alive and well. The Allied mission to Tito's underground confirmed the message. Unfortunately, for some unknown reason, this vital piece of information never got to Allied Command Headquarters in Bari, Italy with heartbreaking consequences for the airmen's families back home.

On April 26, more than three weeks after Joe had been shot down, Rose Roberts received a cryptic cablegram from the Western Union office in Washington, D.C. It bore the message she had always been dreading. Joe's friend, Angelo DiMartino, Seaman First Class with the USCG, was home in Norfolk when the devastating news arrived.

"I just got home on leave and went to see if Joe's mom had received any word from him," he recalls. "When I walked in, everyone was crying and they said 'look on the dining room table'. There on the table was the telegram that said Joe was missing in action. The family was devastated."

The message was short and to the point. Dated 6:47 p.m., April 26, 1944, the cable was from the Adjutant General's office of the US Army. Coached in stilted bureaucratic language, it was as short on information as it was on compassion. "The Secretary of War desires me to express his deep regret that your son, Staff Sgt. Joseph L. Maloney has been reported missing in action since April 2 over Austria," it stated. "If further details or other information are received you will be promptly notified."

On the delicate matter of who exactly was expected to pay for the telegram, there was one other notation: "Delivery charge paid by the government." The exact amount was, however, blacked out on Rose's copy. Nice touch. She never forgave the government for being so crass.

The following morning, the *Winsted Evening Citizen* dutifully reported that Joe Maloney had become Norfolk's first casualty of the war. The article also mentioned that Joe had pretty much followed in his family's footsteps.

"Sergeant Maloney's uncle, Paul Bouchet, who was a member of Company M from Winsted, was the second man from Norfolk to be killed in the First World War," the story went on to explain. "He died as a result of gas poisoning. His stepfather's brother, Joseph Roberts, was the first Norfolk resident to die in the Great War."

Once again, Norfolk was in mourning. Flags were lowered to half staff at the Roberts-Bouchet Branch of the American Legion on Memorial Green, while friends and neighbors tried to console the grief stricken family. To make matters worse, the timing of the news couldn't have been worse. The day after the telegram arrived, Rose received two dozen yellow roses, her favorite, from Joe as an Easter gift. With the flowers came the simple message: "Doing okay. Don't worry about a thing. Love, Your Son."

Joe had ordered the flowers through the American Red Cross in Lecce the day before he left for Steyr. Now, far from bringing her any warmth or comfort, the beautiful bouquet served only as a grim reminder that everything was far from okay with her son.

CHAPTER NINE

Secret Agents, Spies and Strange Bedfellows

Though we observe the Higher Law
And though we have our quarrel just,
Were I permitted to withdraw
You wouldn't see my arse for dust. —
A soldier's verse

Never once expecting a thing in return, the Partisans shared everything they had with their new flying friends. Their food. Their clothes. Even their boots, which Joe gladly accepted even if they were a bit too big. Anything was better than the miserable things he had on his feet. Made of light felt material with a rubber sole, his flight boots were little more than a glorified pair of slippers. Lightweight, comfortable and warm, the electrically heated "booties" were great in the aircraft but absolute murder on the rough ground. Real leather felt good on Joe's tired and bruised feet.

When they bailed out, most of the crew, including Joe, had nothing more on than their flimsy electrical flying suits. The bright blue coveralls stuck out like a soar thumb. Switching to the more practical brown and gray wools of their hosts not only let the airmen blend in with everybody else, but also added immensely to their comfort for the chilly spring nights ahead. There was a measure of self-preservation in the Partisans' generosity. Without proper protection against the elements and the rough terrain, the airmen would soon become exhausted, throwing the whole escape attempt into serious jeopardy. Speed and stealth were everything.

"Actually, it was the Germans who gave us most of our clothes," quips Joe. The Partisans made a regular habit of raiding enemy camps for the things they needed most: guns, food, medicine and any clothing they could get their hands on. They were afraid of nothing. They were particularly fond of attacking German foot patrols. Following a group of enemy soldiers through the woods, they would wait for one of the men to stop to relieve himself.

"That's when they would jump him, slit his throat and strip him of everything," Joe adds. "The Germans became quite unnerved by this type of thing and would often avoid the woods in areas they didn't control."

At other times, the Partisans would capture a German soldier, strip him to his underwear and send him back to his unit, where he would be re-outfitted. If that same soldier were unlucky enough, the Partisans would capture him again and the whole cycle would be repeated. They rarely missed any opportunity to add to their cache.

By the end of their third day in Podgrad, pressure was building for the American airmen to leave. A column of Germans, 300 to 400 strong, in addition to their White Guard lackeys, had already been spotted closing in on several Partisan strongholds in the hills not far from the village. Partisan intelligence was seldom, if ever, wrong.

Determined not to let the bomber crew slip through their dragnet again, the Germans came spoiling for a fight. The 14th SS Panzer Division, one of Hitler's crack units brought in from the battlefields of Italy, were out for blood. Tanks from Novo Mesto were rolling through the nearby villages of Gornje and Spodnje Kakouice, coiled to strike. Soon, light artillery was

Slovenija Partisans marching, 1944. Men like these helped to save Joe and his crew.

added to the deadly German arsenal. Together, they began to pound shells directly into Partisan positions at the very edge of Podgrad. Sitting on the back steps of the church high on the hill, some of Joe's crew watched the action unfold through binoculars. Joe could see the anxiety building in the Partisans' eyes. The Germans were never more than a mile to a mile and a half away from Podgrad ever since the airmen arrived.

But the nightmare that threatened to engulf Podgrad quickly fizzled. While the Cankarjeva Brigada fought brilliantly to stem the enemy's frontal assault, the 15th Bela Krajina Brigade managed to slip in behind the German lines. Caught in a trap, the enemy broke ranks and fled, leaving behind 40 of their dead. Many more were captured, including two officers. By the end of the hour long battle, the Partisans had lost only four men. The Germans had taken a terrific pasting.

Taking advantage of all the confusion, a small group of Partisans managed to slip away with their frightened airmen in tow. They didn't have much time to put some much needed distance behind them. The Germans would be back. Of this they were certain.

As the fading sun doled out its last miserly rays of the late afternoon, Joe and his buddies glanced back at Podgrad for the last time. Darkness quickly fell. All night long they walked wordlessly. Still nursing soar ankles, Fred Streicher was lucky enough to be riding on a horse drawn cart that carried some of their meager supplies. An old beaten down cow path that cut through the hilly countryside led their way. The half dozen Partisans assigned to guide and protect the airmen carried their German and Italian made rifles and machine guns like trophies.

It took a lot of blind trust for Joe and the others to put their lives in the hands of complete strangers that first night. By now they better understood the name Tito and the red star on the Partisans caps. They represented communism, the sworn enemy, just like fascism, of every free and democratic country in the world. Joe chuckled at the strange irony of this new friendship. War was indeed mad.

At first light the next morning, the Germans blasted their way back into Podgrad to even the score as the Partisans knew they would. This time it was the Luftwaffe's turn to dish out the punishment. Stanislav Erjavec, having already delivered his message to the Fourth Battalion at Mrasevo, was on his way into the village when the attack came.

"Seventeen Stuka dive bombers zoomed in low from over the hills," he gestures with hands punching the air. As it turned out, it was one of the strangest attacks he had ever seen. Bombs were going off all over the place, but only one of them actually hit the village itself, and, for some reason, that one didn't even go off.

The 300 kilogram bomb had glanced off the church steeple and plunged into the ground. It turned out to be a dud. A lucky break. At that very moment over 200 Partisans were next door in the rectory holding a meeting. Had the bomb gone off, they wouldn't have had a chance. The loss of so many soldiers at once would have severely jeopardized the balance of power in the liberated territory of Bela Krajina, not to mention the impact it would have had on the fate of any downed Allied airmen trying to escape in the future. Podgrad counted its blessings, thankful for the poor marksmanship and even worse luck of its enemy.

Several civilians were killed in the surrounding hills, including a family of three in a farmhouse in nearby Konc. However, Alojz Murn, secretary of the Slovenija Liberation Front for the District of Podgrad, quickly determined that most of the peasants had escaped safely into the woods. After regrouping, there was much celebration that night with extra portions of Slivovitz, the national drink of homemade plum brandy, for everyone. Podgrad was never again attacked with such vengeance.

The first couple of days of their flight to freedom were rough on Joe and his crew. They walked expeditiously at night and slept fitfully by day, always on edge for the slightest sign of trouble. The forced silence at night was the worst part for Joe. Talking was forbidden. When words were absolutely necessary, they were spoken in low whispered tones. The airmen were warned never to cough, laugh or sneeze out loud. The same went for belching and farting. Not helping matters any was the fact that the first few nights were crisp and cold, ideal conditions for the slightest sound to travel for miles around.

The rules about unnecessary noise made perfect sense. After all, why would they want to advertise their presence to the enemy? But, stealth came at a high price. Just when they needed to draw together for emotional support during the long, dangerous walks at night, the airmen were forced to keep quiet, with only their frightened inner thoughts to keep them company. The isolation soon began to jangle the group's raw nerves. Joe noticed the effects on the more outgoing and talkative ones like John Reilly

Typical Slovenija Partisan Brigade on the move through enemy territory of Yugoslavia.

and the usually irrepressible William Kollar. In their emotional prison, they became fidgety and easily irritated. It was not a good sign.

Things were not a whole lot better by day either, when they slept, or, at least tried to. Their beds were little more than fir branches spread over the cold, hard ground. Sometimes, if they were really lucky, they bedded down in a haymow in some out-of-the-way barn, always making sure the farmer and his family were never around. "Keeping warm when we slept was a real problem," Joe says. "It was early spring and the days were still cold and damp. Whenever we found a cow in one of the barns, she always had lots of company. They made excellent foot warmers."

After the first few nights, Joe's feet began to crack and bleed from painful blisters. His ill-fitting boots, no match for the quick pace of their forced march, were beginning to take their toll. But, he had to press on. No room for slackers in this outfit. The tempo wasn't set by the slowest one among them. This was a race, pure and simple. Finally, after several more grueling days, the Partisans decided to sojourn at a village. For Joe's wretched feet, it wasn't a moment too soon.

Satisfied with the distance they were putting between themselves and the Germans, the guides stopped for more than just some much needed rest. They also had to stock up on food, the first indication Joe had that he was going to be in this for the long haul. The rag-tag soldiers had enough money to buy a few supplies, mostly cornmeal, for the group of 16 hungry men. Their other stores like bread, potatoes, a few onions, and even a bottle of Slivovitz were freely offered by the villagers.

As Joe bit into a piece of leathery pumpernickel bread that evening, his thoughts turned to the plight of a man he had met just the day before. It had been a brief encounter at another village where they had stopped for water but an encounter, nevertheless, that had left him deeply troubled. "The man told me he had lived in the United States before the war and had saved $15,000 after years of driving a beer wagon in Milwaukee," Joe explains. "With his life savings, a substantial amount at the time, he returned to Yugoslavia and opened a general store in early 1939."

The man went on to tell Joe that he had to burn down his own store just the week before to keep it from falling into the hands of the Germans who were sweeping through the valley. With the strike of a single match, his entire life's savings and future went up in smoke. He wept like a baby. The poor man was heartbroken. It was another hard lesson of war. Joe began to feel a little less sorry for himself as he swallowed the last of his bread. At least he could still count on one thing. His home would still be there in Connecticut, if he ever got back to civilization. It was at least something to cling to.

After polishing off his piece of bread, Joe turned his attention to his miserable feet. Blistered and bleeding, there was little he could do but try to stay off them as much as possible. A tall order, considering. A woman gave him some clean strips of cloth for bandages to control the bleeding and ease his pain. Joe felt lucky to be surrounded by such obliging people. Little did he know, luck had very little to do with it.

The Partisans knew the countryside like the backs of their hands and who to trust and who not to. Most peasants in the hills of Yugoslavia were their support group for shelter, food, medicine and information on enemy strength and activities. But not all. Some places had to be avoided like the plague. Knowing who to trust was the trick. Without cooperative villagers, Joe and his crew wouldn't have had a chance.

"Our guides had an incredible communications system," says Joe, "because the villagers who supported Tito always knew when we were coming. If they rang their church bells, it was safe for us to enter. If there were no bells, we would slip by the village unnoticed."

The Partisans had also found another sure fire way of keeping their escape routes as safe and secure as possible. The guides were changed frequently. New faces popped up every couple of days to lead the crew, while familiar faces disappeared silently into the night.

"I finally figured it out," Joe recalls. "They changed guides whenever we went from one Partisan control zone to the next. That's how they always knew every turn of the path, every village, practically every man and woman along the way. Local control was key to their escape operations."

On April 8, almost a week after being shot down, the band of escapees was on the move again. Within hours they found themselves cautiously approaching a dirt airstrip. Little more than a meadow with the rocks picked clean, it was, nevertheless, flat enough to accommodate a light cargo plane with ease. The field straddled the border between southern Slovenija and Croatia. They had made good time. For a change the Partisan guides had decided to risk walking during broad daylight to speed things up. It was late in the afternoon as the airmen waited for the next shoe to drop.

The nearby village of Primostek lay among the sprawling grasslands of a deep, wide valley. Relatively isolated from the rest of the countryside, it was an ideal spot for a rescue attempt. Word quickly spread that an Allied plane from Italy would be coming in that night to take them out. It couldn't be this easy, Joe thought to himself, hoping of course he were wrong. But their chance of an early escape quickly faded as they lay quietly in the bushes, only a stone's throw away from the rough airstrip.

In the never ending seesaw battle for control, it was now the enemy's turn to have the upper hand in the surrounding farmland. Joe and his buddies were too late, probably by no more than a day or so. The Germans had taken over the whole area. It was like that in this type of war where the front changed often, sometimes daily. From his vantage point, Joe could clearly see a number of enemy soldiers pacing back and forth across the meadow, protecting their new prize. Although he knew it had been a long shot, he cursed his bad luck anyway. Dejected, the airmen had no choice but to accept their bitter fate and withdraw.

Step by cautious step, they snaked their way back to the seclusion of a wooded patch along the edge of the meadow. There was nothing for them to do now but wait as one of the guides struck out in search of the fastest and safest way out of the valley. Each man nursed his own anxieties, not unreasoned, over just what it would take to win his freedom. The darkening landscape mirrored their somber mood as the cloak of another twilight fell.

Several hours passed. Not a sign of the guide. Tension was rising. Then, finally, the Partisan reappeared, with hands waving in wild excitement, as if holding back some big secret.

"We followed him up out of the valley in single file," Joe declares. "No one said a word. We trudged along until we came to a small village. Then we understood why he was so excited." Joe was hoping for nothing more than a good meal, or, at the very least, a decent place to sleep. But, what he discovered was much more than that. His heart jumped at the sight before him. Standing in a clearing was a large group of Allied soldiers and airmen.

There was no time to explain as the legion of 81 men was quickly organized into small, more manageable groups. It was obvious to Joe that this was some sort of staging area along the Partisan escape route. He guessed correctly that most of the men were downed British, Canadian and American flyers, like himself, while the rest were likely escaped prisoners of war from all over occupied Europe and north Africa. They also happened to be the largest number of Allied men ever to be assembled by Tito's forces. Their rendezvous took place in southeastern Slovenija, near the towns of Ceremolji and Metlika.

One other thing was obvious to Joe. He noticed that quite a few of the Partisan soldiers hanging around were carrying heavy machine guns and had grenades hanging from their belts. He didn't have to wonder why. The extra firepower spelled only one thing, big trouble ahead! Just how 81 desperate and unarmed men could be kept hidden from the enemy boggled Joe's mind. But, a gallant attempt was going to be made, that was for sure.

"We were split up into units of five men, each flanked by a couple of guides," says Joe. "In this way there was less chance of us all getting killed if we were attacked."

They walked up into the surrounding mountains as night fell, each group separated by a hundred feet or so. This was anything but a seat-of-the-pants operation, Joe thought. The Partisans were well organized.

The column trundled along for hours under clear starlit skies, over steep wooded ridges and across frigid mountain streams. Except for the echo of their boots against the hard ground, they didn't make a sound. A faint haze hugged the ground as the first rays of dawn sliced through the breaking dawn. Wading across a narrow section of the Kolpa River at sunrise, the group left Slovenija behind. A quick change of guides told Joe they were now in Croatia, where an even more ominous threat awaited them.

Croatia was different and much more menacing than the other principalities that made up Yugoslavia. A political struggle between the Serbs and Croats before the war had ended with the Croats withdrawing from the federal parliament in Belgrade. In 1939, on the eve of World War II, Croatia was granted considerable autonomy.

The Fascist, pro-Nazi Croatian separatist group, the Ustashi, had seized power in Zagreb and in April 1941, it established the so called Independent State of Croatia. By 1944, Croatia was occupied by the German army and quickly became the puppet state of the Third Reich. The underworld of the Ustashi had an unparalleled reputation for naked savagery, far exceeding that of its neighbors to the north, the White Guard. No one among the escapees could afford to relax now. Not even for a moment.

Joe and his crew had been told some awful stories about the Ustashi. Even Hitler was said to have been appalled at the methods they employed. They chopped off noses, ears, breasts and limbs. They poured salt into wounds, gouged out eyes and burned and buried their victims alive. Their weapons of choice were hammers, ropes, clubs, fire and bare hands. Bullets were too quick. Only the Germans employed such methods, to the everlasting derision of the Ustashi.

Two bloodthirsty stories in particular always turned Joe's stomach. As he crossed the Kolpa River into Croatia, he recounted every terrifying detail he had learned back in Italy. In the first incident, an Orthodox priest was half buried in the ground while the Ustashi danced around him, slicing off pieces of flesh with their knives. In another account, a mother was forced to hold a bucket to catch the blood of her four children while they were being slaughtered.

Even if the stories were only half true, which Joe tended to doubt, he still regarded the Ustashi as the meanest of the mean in the valley. Crossing the Kolpa River was one of his darkest hours.

The first rest stop for the group of 81 was a brief one, no more than five or six minutes. Joe sat on the soggy ground nursing his tortured feet. In the distance, the snow-covered mountains glistened under the radiant morning sun. The crisp azure sky seemed endless. For one glorious moment, the war was suddenly far away. Sprigs of soft verdant grass reminded him of springtime back home. His thoughts drifted off. Were the daffodils up yet in front of his mother's house? And what about the snow in Connecticut? Had it melted from the well-worn path to his grandfather's chicken coop?

The name Sam Tierney also crept into his consciousness. A fighter pilot with the Mighty 8th in England, his buddy would soon be shot down and captured, to become a prisoner for the rest of the war. But, for the moment, Joe had only pleasant thoughts of his pal because he was still home, if only in his daydream. He and Sam had been real close through the years. The budding flora at Joe's feet reminded him of the great time the two of them had while growing up in Norfolk, especially one night.

Sam's father was a devoted caretaker on one of the town's finest estates. He took particular pride in his rose bushes. Over supper one evening, Sam's father made the mistake of mentioning that his carefully nurtured roses would be in full bloom the very next day. Staring temptation in the face, Sam eagerly met Joe that night for a little adventure. The next day, Sam's father was in a frenzy. His roses were gone. Every last one of them. On the other hand, two young men from Norfolk had made quite an impression on more than a few young ladies with armfuls of beautiful long stem red roses. Joe caught himself smiling as he looked down at his throbbing feet.

"Pokret!" The order to get moving rang out. Not a minute too soon as far as Joe was concerned. His lice infested clothes were starting to get to him. As long as he was on the move, the constant itching was at least tolerable. But, whenever he sat still for any length of time, his clothes came alive. Despite this misery, he was pleased about one thing that morning. Fred Streicher was finally back on his feet, walking on his own down the narrow path in front of his crew like the true leader he was.

The mangy caravan shrugged off fatigue and ignored hunger while enduring several more long hours of tedious walking. They didn't talk. There was always a Ustashi around and English would be like a red flag.

Early in the afternoon, they came upon a cluster of stone cottages. Out from one of them stepped an Allied officer, wearing a well-pressed uniform, polished shoes and sporting a black patch over one eye. The officer snapped to ramrod attention and offered a salute to his surprised guests. Then, he introduced himself. He was, he said, Major William Jones, an emissary from the British to Tito. By his full dress uniform, he had obviously been expecting company. Once again, Joe marveled over the Partisan's incredible early warning system.

Major Jones immediately launched into a quick history lesson. A year earlier, he told the assembled men, the Allies had been backing the Chetniks under General Mihajlovic with increasing dissatisfaction. Escaping airmen and prisoners of war had been bringing back reports for months about a more effective underground movement known as the Partisans. By early 1943 the Allies had to send someone into Yugoslavia to find out exactly what was going on.

That someone was William Jones. Nearly 50 years old at the time, he

Major Wm. Jones (man in front row with cap) at the first session of the Slovenija National Liberation Army Congress held at Crnomelj, Slovenia. Feb. 19-20, 1944.

had lost an eye in the trenches of the Great War. A seasoned veteran of the Black Watch of Canada, the native of Bear River, Nova Scotia was also carrying around some German shrapnel in his legs. All that had earned him the rare Distinguished Conduct Medal and Bar for conspicuous gallantry. But, by 1939, could he fight another war? He was the kind of man who would not take no for an answer.

When Hitler blitzed across Europe at the beginning of World War II, Jones kissed his wife good-bye and went off to Ottawa, fully realizing that his age, not to mention his glass eye and the shrapnel he was wearing, were formidable obstacles to a new military career. Even though he had memorized all the letters on the eye chart in the recruitment office beforehand, a suspicious doctor placed a lighted candle in front of each eye. After getting a normal reaction in one, the doctor tried the other. He moved the candle so close to Jones' glass eye that he singed his eyebrows. The doctor was furious. Canada, Jones was told, didn't need any one-eyed soldiers.

Deciding he might have a better chance of getting into the war in England, Jones, either through dumb luck or by sheer determination, was eventually accepted into the British Army's Special Services Branch with the rank of major. He soon became head of the first Allied mission into Yugoslavia. He was a secret agent, part of a world-wide intelligence network set up by British Prime Minister Winston Churchill.

Canadians like Jones who became secret agents served with the British organization called the Special Operations Executive or SOE. Specially trained SOE agents were smuggled into Occupied Europe where they linked

up with members of local Resistance movements, trained them, and organized them into a fighting force to weaken the enemy before the Allied
advance. By 1944 the SOE had almost 14,000 operatives in the occupied
countries of Europe and Asia.

At precisely 1:00 a.m., May 19, 1943, Major Jones, wearing the uniform of his old regiment the Blackwatch, 13th Canadian Battalion, stepped
out of an airplane and into the moonlit night at the end of a parachute. With
his ripcord dangling on his chest, he wondered if the thing would work.
After all, it was his first jump.

"My, it was such a beautiful night over the Balkans," Joe heard him
recall. "The countryside looked like home, like Nova Scotia."

Jones, code-named "Lawrence of Yugoslavia," landed in Krvatska Palje,
the heart of Croatia, where he joined up with the Partisans. He was soon
impressed with what he saw. At their command camp, he found a hydro
plant and a fully tooled machine shop performing precision repairs on heavy
weapons. There were even bandage and clothing factories and a steam bath.
All this was hidden under the trees and had been operating for more than a
year within sight of a major German army depot. He wrote up a glowing
report for his superiors back in England.

The Canadian major was instrumental in persuading Prime Minister
Churchill that Tito, and no one else, was the man to back in the Balkans.
From then on Jones lived with the Partisans in the mountains and in their
caves. He spoke fluent German and was trusted implicitly by all those around
him. While no one in Yugoslavia was clear about the exact nature of Jones'
duties, he was known to have worked all over the Balkans in fighting the
Germans. He gained a reputation as one of the most enthusiastic and ardent
supporters of the Partisan's cause.

"He told us he was here to coordinate Allied air drops and to help people
like us get back home," Joe says. "The major pleaded with us to follow the
Partisans without question." That's just what the band of escapees needed
to hear at this point. Major Jones offered them one other piece of interesting information. He would be joining them on their walk for the next little
while.

"That does it," Joe whispered to John Reilly. "There's gonna be real
trouble up ahead."

April 13th. So far so good, in spite of the heightened sense of danger.
The flight to freedom was proceeding without any major hitches except for
a couple of awful smelling Russians who had mysteriously turned up in
their midst one night.

They were spies for Joseph Stalin. Nobody, not even the Partisan guides,
were happy about the arrangement but it seemed there was little anyone
could do about it. The Russians obviously still had some clout in the Balkans.
"The man and woman were a search and record team," Joe soon learned.

"While one of them questioned the Partisans about the enemy's strength and movements, as well as their own, the other one would write the information down in a notebook. They were especially interested in us airmen, where we had come from, and where we were going."

It was intelligence gathering, Russian army style. Efficient but very unfriendly. The pair gave everybody the creeps, especially after what happened one night.

"A small group of us was sleeping on the floor of an abandoned house. We were packed in like sardines," Joe remembers, "Somebody rolled over against the woman by accident. She freaked out and started yelling and screaming so hard that I thought we were under attack."

After she calmed down, Joe knew no one was trying to molest her. She stank too hard for that. Besides, the Partisans would have killed anybody caught having sex. The rules about this were clear. There was no room for making babies in this outfit.

After a few days, the two Russians disappeared as mysteriously as they had arrived. Everyone was relieved, especially Major Jones. Fostering closer relations between Tito and the Allies was tough enough without interference from the Russians. Joseph Stalin was increasingly on the outs with his Allied partners and Churchill didn't trust him. Neither did Jones. "It's a wonder the Partisans didn't kill them before they had a chance to slip away," Joe says. "But it was good riddance and we never saw their smelly hides again."

Joe would soon learn that not all intruders would be so lucky. Especially when it came to one young Ustashi soldier who also turned up in their midst.

CHAPTER TEN

The Price of Freedom

Fast falls the eventide;
The darkness deepens.
Swift to its close
Ebbs out life's little day.

> Abide With Me
> Henry Francis Lyte (1793-1847)

The next few days were a roller coaster ride. The weary airmen and escaped POWs walked, ran and walked some more. They rested in five minute spurts whenever they could. Their clothes drooped limply from their gaunt frames. Their frenetic pace served as a constant reminder of the danger they faced at every turn. But the worst part for Joe was never knowing what was really going on from one moment to the next.

"We knew by instinct that the Germans were hot on our heels," he says, "but that was all. We were helpless when it came to protecting ourselves. We had no control over our lives and that was very frightening."

True to form, the Partisans kept tight lipped about their plans. Their strategy was simple. Secrecy meant security. Major Jones did not interfere either. He knew Tito's soldiers were boss and their way was never to reveal anything. That was just fine with him. He was only interested in results. How the Partisans did their job was their business. At one point Joe did overhear the major mention something about a place up ahead where there would be a radio to contact the 15th Army Air Force Base in Bari,

Italy, presumably to arrange their evacuation. But where this place was or how long it would take to get there, Major Jones was not about to reveal to anyone.

At this stage of the escape attempt, the 81 men were scattered all over the place in small groups. While they traveled a parallel course, they were separated by miles of wilderness. Joe felt uneasy about this. John Reilly felt the same, and kept complaining that he was still not having a good day. It became their inside joke.

By 1944 Germany was well aware of its changing fortunes in Yugoslavia. With things going badly on their other fronts as well, they had even more reason to strike hard against the Partisans. The Axis had to stop the hemorrhaging somewhere and the Balkans was as good a place to start as any.

The German High Command had put a price on Jones' head, 10,000 gold marks. They circulated wanted posters and wrote his name into the "White Book" of Partisans and Allies to be liquidated. The Canadian with the glass eye, who never smoked, drank or swore, and always carried a Bible in his hip pocket was a marked man. Those who associated with him were in just as much danger.

On the morning of April 19, Joe and the 20 or so other men in his group shuffled into a village of rustic stone houses clustered in the middle of a hill rimmed basin. Having walked all night, they were exhausted and hungry. But, their mood was surprisingly upbeat. Word quickly spread that eggs and pancakes would be served for breakfast, thanks to the kind villagers. It sure beat another helping of cornmeal. One of the women even told Art Fleming that hot chocolate was on the menu. What luck!

"The weird thing about the lady who told me this," Art remembers, "was that she spoke very good English and knew a lot about the United States."

He was dumbfounded to learn that she had not only lived in the United States at one time, but had also settled in Pittsburgh, his hometown. Like the unfortunate man Joe had met earlier, the

Slovenija woman peeling potatoes for Partisans. Many of Joe's meals came from the villagers while he was on the run from the enemy.

122

one who had to burn down his own store, she too had returned to Yugoslavia just before the war and was now forced to stay.

Just as Joe and the rest of the men began to settle into a breakfast fit for a king, a German foot patrol was quietly slipping into the other end of the village. An alert lookout smelled the trap before it was sprung.

"Pokret," came the shrill order. "We scattered into the woods just as a bunch of small spotter planes came swooping down with machine guns blazing," Joe says. "They even started to throw some hand grenades at us."

Joe darted from tree to tree to get out of the line of fire. The attack went on and on, as did Joe's dance in the forest to stay alive.

As one plane broke off the attack to refuel, another one took its place. Tree branches snapped and the ground heaved under a steady rain of bullets and explosions. It was going to be a long day. Joe thanked God for a big oak tree as he watched one of his buddies dive for cover under a pile of brush, bullets nipping at his heels.

At around noon it was all over. The planes suddenly disappeared. The silence was almost deafening. There was no sign of the enemy foot patrol either. Staggering from his hiding place, Joe blinked in the bright sunlight as the others slowly gathered around him. It was time to count noses.

Miraculously, every one in the group emerged from the protective cover of the forest unscathed, including the guides. There was no time to celebrate, however. After regrouping, they decided to take their chances in the open. The eggs and pancakes would have to wait as they hightailed it down a long, wide road, kicking up small dust storms with every hasty step.

No more than a half hour later another obstacle stood in their way, a burly JU-88. It came out of the blue at about 2,000 feet. The JU-88 was nothing to mess with as Joe had already learned the hard way. While the British Spitfire could outmaneuver anything; the American P-51 Mustang could outrun just about everybody; and the P-47 Thunderbolt was as tough as nails when it took a hit, the JU-88 was a wolf in wolf's clothing. Their young pilots were still among the best, even after the Luftwaffe had lost control of the skies over Europe. Maybe that's why they had something extra to prove. Joe broke into a cold sweat and his knees went to jelly as he fought a powerful urge to heave his gut out.

"We dove into the ditches," he says, "and lay there like stacked cordwood with nothing but open fields all around us."

Joe fought back the urge to look up, even though the Partisans had always warned him not to. The oil on his face would reflect sunlight and make him one hell of an easy target. He also suppressed a mad desire to scratch his itchy hide. His lice were working overtime from all his warm sweat. He cursed the miserable little bastards through clenched teeth.

"John Reilly and I were next to each other as usual," says Joe. "He reached over and I grabbed his hand. We were thinking the same thing."

"This is it," Reilly's voice cracked in a half whisper. "I'll see you in the next place, Heaven or Hell. I'm still not having a good day."

Joe didn't know whether to laugh to cry. Their little inside joke suddenly sounded pathetic. Panic-stricken, Joe held his breath. He could hear the dull drone of the Junkers in the distance slowly build into a piercing roar as it whipped by overhead. He took another deep breath and waited for the awful roar to come back. Seconds passed. Then, the air was dead quiet. Joe slowly raised his sweat soaked forehead and took a peek. So did the others. The coast was clear!

Incredibly, the enemy pilot hadn't seen them. Maybe the young studs of the Luftwaffe were not so hot after all. Or just maybe the men on the ground had done one wicked impression of a pile of cordwood. Either way, Joe was relieved to be breathing again and John Reilly was glad to get another chance to have a good day.

The haggard looking bunch of men scrambled out of their would be graves. There was no time to waste. They knew the Germans were still out there somewhere. Joe was also worried about the Ustashi. Out in the open, the airmen were easy prey for the collaborators who could be anywhere and everywhere along the way. They were in Bosnia now, having crossed the border from Croatia about an hour earlier. Borders meant nothing to the Ustashi. They could be just as vicious on either side.

At about mid afternoon the troop ran smack into another problem. This time, it was Mother Nature calling the shots. A river, only a stone's throw across, but, too deep from all the spring runoff for wading, blocked their path. Even more worrisome was the enemy scout plane that kept zipping up and down the river. This time, the enemy was one step ahead of them.

As they gathered on the riverbank, the Partisans came up with an idea. The plan was risky but they had no other choice. Besides, they couldn't go back now, after coming so far. It was straight ahead or nothing at this point.

"We were taken to a farmhouse next to the river so we could keep out of sight," Joe says with a wry grin. "Then the guides clocked the plane each time it made a pass. They soon figured out how much time we needed to get across the river without being noticed."

The farmer took three men across at a time in his rowboat. He had enough time to row back, turn his boat over on the riverbank and hide in the bushes before the plane reappeared. This way everything always looked the same to the pilot. It took the rest of the afternoon, but every man made it safely to the other side.

With daring and ingenuity, the Partisans had outfoxed the Germans once more. They also had a bit of luck on their side. Seems their farmer friend was sitting on both sides of the fence. According to Major Jones, who had all kinds of Allied intelligence at his disposal, the man was not exactly an angel of mercy. More like a mercenary. Trusted by both the

Partisans crossing the Kolpa River. Joe and his group made it across this river in a row boat – three at a time.

Partisans and the Germans, he had the reputation of helping one side one day and the other the next. Once again, Joe couldn't help but think just how crazy war could be.

After regrouping on the other side of the river, the men were in for a royal treatment. Three army trucks were waiting for them. Just where they came from, nobody bothered to ask. They sped along for a good hour or so before lurching to a stop. It was too dangerous to keep going by night. The headlights and engine noise would give them away. It was to be their only ride. There was one consolation at the end of their day though. It was time to eat, the first time in over 20 hours.

After forcing down his umpteenth bowl of cornmeal, Joe finished up with a crust of bread so tough it made his jaws ache. At least it was something to put in his stomach, even though he could no longer ignore the need to tighten his belt every couple of days. Still hungry, he longed for the delicious smell of the bakery back at the base.

Life in Lecce now seemed easy by comparison. Everyday, Joe and some of the guys would lie in wait for the warm loves of freshly baked bread to be carried across the compound from the bakery to the mess. The Italians who ran the bakeshop under a special arrangement with the United States military always objected, but the boys helped themselves anyway.

For an extra treat, Joe liked to wash down the still warm bread with a bottle of Asti Spumante sparkling wine. It was usually available at the PX for a buck. The U.S. Army had taken over the winery at Pessoni, Italy and all the bottling was done under American military supervision to make sure it was safe to drink. Nice touch, Joe mused, as he stretched out to give his tortured feet a rest. His hunger pangs refused to go away, but he thanked God for the little food that he did have, and for the fact that, no matter how little there was to go around, the Partisans always made sure he and the others ate first. Always!

Late that night it was time to move on. A brisk walk brought them to another small village in a matter of hours. From there, they immediately struck out to make their way up over a high mountain pass and down into a deep valley where they came across a set of railroad tracks. Their attempt to cross, however, was doomed from the start.

As Joe squatted down behind some bushes, the hair on the back of his neck bristled. He could clearly see a number of German soldiers riding back and forth on the tracks on handcars. Complicating matters was the fact that they were shooting hundreds of phosphorus flares attached to parachutes high into the air, illuminating everything like the noonday sun. The Germans had been expecting them!

There was nowhere to go but back the way they had come, all the way back over the mountain to the village where they had started out. By the time they got back, dawn was already breaking. It was a major disappointment in light of the fact that they had overcome an even greater challenge only a few nights earlier on the Karlovac-Zagreb Road and railroad line.

A major twin corridor for the two way shipment of German troops and supplies, it was naturally heavily patrolled. Trying to get across would be

A Partisan keeping watch over a defensive position. Heavy guns like this were often used to protect American airmen in occupied territory.

dangerous. But, again, there was little choice. Sweating bullets, Joe and the others decided they would try their luck in groups of two.

"When it was my turn to go, I looked over my shoulder where the Partisans had set up a machine gun nest in case of trouble," Joe says. "I'll never forget looking into the face of a very pretty woman."

Joe was both surprised and relieved at the sight of this young soldier, surprised because he couldn't figure out why he had not noticed her good looks before, and relieved because, when it came to Partisan men and women, there was no difference in their ability to fight. Once the 20 or so men made it safely to the other side, they had to crawl on their hands and knees past a building full of sleeping German troops.

"We were so close," Joe chuckles, "that I could hear some of them snoring through an open window."

Unfortunately, it was not a night to be so easily repeated. Back in the village where their latest escape attempt had ground to a halt, the dejected men were split up into small groups to eat and rest in the dozen or so houses. The village was at the closed end of a long horseshoe valley, not the best place for a quick getaway. Despite his uneasy feelings about a trap, Joe settled in, hoping for the best. It was around 8 o'clock on the morning of April 20.

"Four of us were with an old peasant woman," Joe says. "She started roasting some potatoes and warming up a can of milk for our breakfast. We could hardly wait."

He felt bad for the poor woman, but he couldn't keep his eyes off the browning spuds that he knew would soon be his. His memory reached back, touching echoes of a time when, as a young lad, he used to help his grandmother Minnie fix breakfast over her hot kitchen stove. For another brief moment, Joe forgot the terror that constantly clutched at his heart. But only for a moment. Reality was always just around the corner.

He couldn't help but notice how primitive the house was: dirt floor, no furniture to speak of, not even a stove or chimney. An open wood fire in the middle of the floor served as the only source of heat. Wispy columns of smoke rose idly through a hole in the roof. Joe felt both humble and grateful. He knew she couldn't spare the food, but he had not eaten in over 36 hours. He could hardly wait for his first bite as he felt the deep rumble of his empty stomach.

Just as the sparse offerings were about to be served, the roof and walls of the house reverberated with the report of gunfire. It was the familiar rat-tat-tat of enemy machine guns. Joe's eyes shot skyward as the roof was raked with bullets. He knew the bloody Germans had to be just outside the door by the sound of things.

"Run for it!" Joe shouted to the others as he bolted out the door.

The men stumbled in a blind panic across a newly plowed field. Their feet sank into the fresh spring soil with every step, slowing their escape. Bill Kollar nearly lost a boot. That would have been it for him. Joe didn't stop to look around for the old lady. He knew it was no use, as a sickening pang of guilt and anger rushed over him.

"As we ran up a hill towards the woods, I heard a loud burst of gunfire coming from right in front of us," Joe says. "That's when I realized the whole mountainside at the closed end of the valley was ringed with Germans and Ustashi. We were trapped."

There was only one way out. They would have to turn around and run straight down the middle of the entire valley to get to the open end. The ring of fire was an unbelievable distance of two to three miles. Bullets and mortar shells drizzled at their feet as they began to run like they never ran before.

"I remember seeing one of the guys, the only Frenchman with us, grab a pair of horses hitched to a wagon he had come across," recalls Joe. "Standing up, he rode it like a Roman chariot at full gallop. When he raced by me he hit a bump and was pitched off."

Good thing. A few seconds later, a mortar shell landed smack between the horses and blew up the whole business. Pieces of horse flesh and splinters of wood rained down everywhere. The Frenchman was one lucky man, more than he could have imagined.

Joe and the others had had their suspicions about him, if for no other reason than no one could understand him. Everybody was paranoid enough without having someone around who spoke a different language. There were whispers that he might be an enemy plant. Joe and John Reilly always made sure the Frenchman walked between them. Joe even carried a club that he had fashioned from a tree branch. If the stranger had made one wrong move, Joe was prepared to kill him. Lucky for both, it never came to that. Only later would Joe learn of the Frenchman's true identity.

Red faced and gasping for breath, Joe ran for all his might, ignoring the searing pain in his feet. At one point he looked over his shoulder and did a double take.

"Art Fleming was the littlest guy in our crew with real short legs," he says. "Yet he went flying past me like I was standing still. The whole thing looked so ridiculous that I nearly fell down laughing."

Even with sore feet, Joe figured he could have outrun Art any day of the week because of the big difference in their height. Obviously he hadn't factored in the influence of blind panic in his buddy.

From high in the hills, Joe could see the flash of the guns and hear the thud of the mortars growing more intense by the minute. The bullet riddled ground quaked under his feet. Sweat burned his eyes. Everything around him was in utter chaos. Not one inch of ground was spared from the enemy's firepower.

With a bloodcurdling shriek, Fred Streicher went down in a heap, the calf of his right leg shattered by a 30 caliber machine-gun bullet. Lagging behind because of his sore ankles, he was an easy target. Falling backwards from the impact, he landed head-first, facing down the rock strewn embankment of a very steep gully. First his pants, then his shirt oozed a deep red as a river of blood washed over him.

"I didn't see Fred get hit," Joe says with a tone of bitterness. "I was ahead of him, but I was told later that Major Jones stopped to apply a tourniquet to slow the bleeding."

Streicher wore a blank expression of shock as he lay bathed in his own warm blood. It actually made him feel cozy in a strange sort of way.

His chest was rising and falling to the rhythm of his quick shallow breaths. He could feel the veins in his temples pounding madly. Streicher opened his eyes. His head spun giddily. He felt like he was going to blackout, but then things steadied a bit and he began to focus. He was conscious, but just barely. His leg wound pressed hard against his pants. He could see fragments of glistening white bone protruding through the flesh and blood. He wanted to vomit to relieve the sickening pain deep within his gut.

After helping him as much as he could, Major Jones pressed on, knowing that Streicher's only chance for survival lay with capture, and, hopefully, medical care by the Germans, if the Ustashi didn't get to him first. In different circumstances, a wounded comrade would always find help and refuge in the nearest Partisan cave before being taken to one of their hospitals hidden deep in the woods. This time, experience told Major Jones that the Partisans could not help. George Morrell thought otherwise. He went back to see what he could do. The 20-year-old knelt over his stricken pilot and began to sob.

"Oh my God! Oh my God! What are we going to do?" he wept openly. "Tell me what to do."

"I'll be okay," came Streicher's hushed reply, fingers pressed tight to his parched lips, fighting for every word. "You have to get the hell out of here. There's nothing you can do for me now. You have to save yourself. Get going!"

Morrell looked around for some water. He could see that Streicher was going into shock. The dry lips and the shallow breathing told him so. There was no water to be found, even if he would have had the time to fetch some.

"I won't leave you!" Morrell choked back.

"Get the hell out of here right now," barked Streicher, knowing the trap his friend was falling into with each passing second.

Morrell finally nodded and reluctantly stood up. Without saying a word he wiped the tears away from his sweat stained cheeks with a tattered sleeve and turned to run. He had barely taken a step when a shot rang out. Morrell stumbled and fell, killed instantly by a bullet through the heart. He never saw it coming. He had been shot in the back at point blank range. Hardly a spot of blood came from the fatal wound as his limp body lay next to his wounded pilot.

Bombardier Clark Fetterman had seen the whole thing from a short distance away. He later recorded his observations in an official report to the USAAF.

"Morrell ran back to try and give him first aid, with the further intention of hiding Lieutenant Streicher behind some rocks until later in the day when it would be safer for us to come back. However, Morrell was surrounded by some of the German patrol who shot him and, after beating Lieutenant Streicher, left them lying on the ground."

This was only the beginning for Streicher. A Ustashi came along minutes later and started beating him senseless with his rifle butt. The blows to his head knocked him out cold. When he came to, he could see the blurred outline of a German soldier methodically going through his pockets, stealing his wallet, cigarettes and watch. The indignity of it all, Streicher thought as he blacked out again.

Despite his perilous situation, Streicher was fortunate that the German soldier had turned up when he did. It probably saved him from a far worse fate at the hands of the vile Ustashi. Besides, what possible use would he have now for his money or watch? His cigarettes were, of course, a different matter. He was dying for a smoke. Again, Fetterman's official report of the incident picks up the story.

"Shortly afterwards, however, some German officers returned and, finding Lieutenant Streicher still alive, dressed him in Morrell's clothes because his own were soaked with blood...and took Lieutenant Streicher with them as a prisoner, leaving Morrell lying shirtless where he had fallen."

As he lay bleeding, Streicher offered only his name, rank and serial number to his captors. He pleaded with the German CO to bury his friend. But, the officer was more interested in the pilot's German sounding name. "Streicher, Streicher," he kept saying in broken English. "How can you bomb your own people?"

"Because I am a soldier following orders just like you" came the defiant reply. The German officer quickly dropped his line of questioning.

With chilling irony, orders promoting George Morrell from Warrant Officer to Second Lieutenant had arrived in Lecce that very day. His promotion went through anyway. Two weeks later, when the army notified Morrell's mother of her son's fate, she dropped dead of a heart attack. Morrell's body was buried in an unmarked spot on the mountainside by the Partisans. The secret location kept the Ustashi from robbing the grave.

As Streicher was being carted away on the back of a horse drawn wagon, he could see a pall of smoke rising over the village in the horseshoe valley

Burning down villages that helped the Partisans was always the German way.

below. He could also hear the crackle of machine guns. He understood only too well what it all meant. The Germans and Ustashi were dishing out their usual deadly verdict against those who had helped the Partisans. The few people they didn't execute on the spot they took for forced labor throughout the Reich, mostly the young and healthy ones. The Ustashi stole the food and killed the livestock. Nothing was spared. What they couldn't take with them they burned to the ground. This was always the way. It was their calling card. Joe cringed at the thought of what must have happened to the kind old lady he had left behind roasting a few potatoes and warming a can of milk for his breakfast. Heartbroken, he had to force himself to press on.

The adrenaline driven men stumbled every torturous step of the way into the forested hills beyond the open end of the valley, out of the enemy's reach. Safe for the moment, they fell silent and tried to cope with the horrible fact that two of their own would not be joining them. Their only consolation was knowing that it could have just as easily been them. They were alive and they had to keep going, no matter what. There was no time to grieve. Joe knew Streicher and Morrell would have wanted it that way.

For the rest of the day and well into the night they doggedly plodded on, their drawn, waif like faces a picture of fierce determination. They hoped and prayed that they could put some distance between themselves and their tormentors. After 50 hours on the run, with virtually nothing to eat, they slunk into an out-of-the-way barn under the cover of darkness. Completely exhausted, they dropped where they stood.

The night was bitterly cold but they hardly notice anymore. The fleas and lice bristled under their grimy clothes, but they no longer cared. All they wanted was sleep, if only to escape the madness. They were at the breaking point.

Faint slivers of morning light beckoned as the Partisan soldiers, who showed so little regard for their own safety the day before, were already preparing another hot meal of polenta. The smell of food was an invitation Joe could not resist, no matter how tired he was.

"It was pure heaven," he recalls, as the cool morning dew licked at his ill fitting boots. "As usual it didn't taste like much because we never had any salt but it kept me going for one more day."

Some of the men retched at their first taste of food in so long. Others had to be coaxed to stay awake long enough to eat. The hasty meal was soon over. Dawn was breaking and they were running the risk of being discovered by the farmer. In this territory, they could trust no one. The guides set a fast pace under a gray and foreboding sky. Everybody struggled to keep up. It was now April 21. Or so Joe thought. He couldn't be sure anymore.

One day slipped into the next as the human train continued to walk and run. They were somewhere in Bosnia, still secure in the knowledge that the Partisans were doing their best to keep them alive. Joe came to know them as men and women of fierce loyalty, a quality equaled only by their hatred of their enemies, especially the Ustashi. He had already seen the results of just how deep that hatred ran after a young collaborator was caught trying to infiltrate the group. Quickly branded a spy, the Partisans showed him no mercy.

"They forced the guy to march beside us until he was completely played out," he recalls. "They kept hitting him in the small of the back with their rifle butts. Each time he fell, they would kick and punch him in the head and stomach and then drag him back up to his feet."

The more he cried out in pain, the more they beat him. The Partisans even offered some of the airmen their rifles so they could join in the slugfest, but they declined.

"I couldn't be that cruel," offers Joe, "even though he was going to turn us in to be tortured and killed."

Although he refused their offers of a rifle, Joe was within easy reach of another weapon, the steel "D" handle from his ripcord. He had wisely stuck the thing in his flight suit on the way down in his parachute. The Partisans had taught him how to turn it into a dagger. He kept it at the ready in case the young Ustashi tried to make a run for it.

Just as the group was getting ready to cross a busy road, a couple of the Partisans took their battered and bleeding prisoner behind a clump of bushes. They knew it was too risky to keep him around in the open. "As I walked

132

by the spot where they were holding him, I heard an ungodly gurgling sound." Joe remembers.

Looking over his left shoulder, he could see a contorted face, a face that was staring sightlessly skyward. Even at 20 feet, Joe could see pools of bright red blood running over the brown earth. A sharp knife to the throat had done the trick. Joe figured the Ustashi spy was no more than 14 years old. Such was the stuff of war.

Although their prisoner was only a lad, the Partisans offered no apologies. Why should they? This was war, total war. Since 1941, bands of Ustashi had been roaming the countryside, leaving one massacre after another behind. Bosnia ran with blood, as Serbian men, women and children were slaughtered, churches desecrated and Orthodox priests murdered. Their young informants and spies decided who would live and who would die. The excesses of the Ustashi, the torturing, raping, burning and drowning of their victims, had but one consequence. The Partisans had to fight fire with fire. This kind of war was dirty and desperate.

After ducking across the wide open road, the rag-tag coalition of airmen and escaped POWs pushed on. They shadowed their guides over endless rolling hills and grasslands flecked with the budding hardwoods of the early spring. There was only one speed of course, full steam ahead, day and night. Joe's feet were killing him. The Partisans provided him with fresh bandages whenever they could, but, at this point, nothing seemed to make much of a difference.

As he took a quick breather one evening, Joe wondered if the Germans would ever give up. He watched the shiny moon peek up over the barren majesty of a distant mountain range. After being stalked for the kill for so long, he found the peace and quiet unsettling. How could there be such an ugly war in such a beautiful place, he asked himself over and over again. Unable to come up with a satisfactory answer, he settled instead for looking for shooting stars. Whenever he saw one, he always seemed to have a good night, free from the menace of his relentless pursuers. Spotting shooting stars not only became his pastime. It quickly became his passion.

The next morning, Joe and the others walked down a mountain path that took them into another village. The church bells were ringing, so it was safe for them to enter. There, Joe found the peace and quiet he had been yearning for in a small country church. It had a dirt floor, plank benches and a tiny altar. He sat down to gather his thoughts and to pray, grateful to be alone for a change, if only for a few minutes. It was quiet, save for the singing of some birds somewhere in the nearby treetops. When it was time to go, the tiny church and the peace it offered were etched into his memory forever.

Tracing a winding path that sloped down into a gorge surrounded by a tapestry of rock faced bluffs rising up from the banks of the Una River,

Drvar, Bosnia, one of the many small towns Joe was taken to by the Partisans during the escape.

they entered the ruins of the once busy Bosnian town of Drvar. There was no mistaking this place. Road signs were everywhere. A feeling of expectation filled the air on the afternoon of April 24th.

This was, after all, Tito's headquarters. He lived in a cave on the rock face, 60 feet above the ground. Drvar was also home to Prime Minister Churchill's son, Randolph, a top British liaison officer assigned to Tito's Fifth Corps Command. The handful of British and American emissaries was a welcome sight. His job finished, Major Jones left the group to return to Slovenija.

Drvar was a busy spot. With the growth of the Partisan movement, Tito's headquarters had expanded rapidly. Besides British, American and Soviet missions, the American Army Air Force had set up a meteorological station there, flying weather balloons into the sky above the town. There were even some dancers in town from the Zagreb Ballet.

Tito's headquarters were neither secret nor mobile, and for good reason. The German Sixth Offensive had already failed to dislodge the Partisans as a tough and efficient fighting force in Yugoslavia; Tito had grown more bold as a result of the increased aid he was receiving from the Allies; and, the Allies had been making good progress on their other fronts as well. But this didn't discourage the Germans who, by now, had more forces in the Balkans than ever before, over 360,000 men in all.

One night, on the eve of his 52nd birthday, Tito lay down after a late meal in his cave to sleep. Hours later, just as it was getting light, he awoke to see two Foche-Wulf aircraft doing low level reconnaissance flights back and forth over the valley. Then, from out of the sun came half a dozen large JU-52s-full of German troops. As enemy parachutes billowed above Drvar, gliders with more men and arms aboard quickly followed. The whole face of the cliff that housed Tito's headquarters came under intense fire.

There was no way out except by way of a waterfall at the back of the cave. Dry at the time, Tito and his men scrambled up a channel that led through a tunnel to the top, even managing to drag Tito's dog, Tiger, up behind them with a rope. Heavily outnumbered, the Partisans regrouped and counterattacked. The German Seventh Offensive failed in its immediate objective, even though the airborne attack was joined the following day by heavy armored forces. By then it was already too late for the Germans. Tito was long gone. So were his headquarters in Drvar. Had Joe and his group arrived a week later, no one would have been around to help them in their escape.

"We stayed in Drvar for a couple of days," Joe adds. "We never got to talk to Tito, so we spent our time scrounging around for food. At night we slept in a bombed out building."

A barber even offered them a free shave. With the fate of the Ustashi spy still fresh on their minds, there was the little matter of trust when it came to someone flashing a straight razor in their faces. But, as usual, the gambler in the group figured he had nothing to lose. Bill Kollar stepped up to the front of the line.

"It sure felt good," Joe says, after his turn in the barber's chair, still trying to ignore the bleeding tangle of festering sores on his feet. Rumor had it that Drvar was the end of the line; that Allied C-47 transports, ferrying supplies to the Partisans from Italy, would be taking them out any day now. Tito's headquarters had already been in radio contact with the 15th Air Force Base in Bari. This must have been the place Major Jones had been talking about, Joe figured. But he knew an evacuation by air couldn't be done from Drvar. The burly terrain made that impossible. The rescue would have to be done from somewhere else. But where? Bari was only a two hour's flight away, but it might as well have been on the far side of the moon at this point. The order came to move out. Joe and the others were off to an airfield, a half day's trek away. The Partisans were more liberal with their information now, an indication the end of their ordeal was near. Struggling up the rock strewn trails leading out of Drvar was bone tiring work, but they were bound and determined to make it the rest of the way.

Joe was soon a lather of sweat. His filthy clothes stuck to his body. Darting through the thick woods, the men eventually came to a stretch of open grasslands. Somewhere out there was a field good enough to call an airstrip and their ticket home. Radio contact was made with Italy from an English outpost in the nearby village of Bosan Petrovac, where the group quickly sought refuge. There they would wait until a plane could get in. It might take days, maybe longer. The Partisans cautioned the boisterous, almost frenetic men not to get too excited. It could be a long haul yet, they were warned, and they needed to keep their wits about them.

"It was nerve wracking," says Joe, "being so close, yet so far. All we could do was pace back and forth, waiting to be sprung from our prison." Joe knew there was no way the Partisans could conceal the grassy strip for very long, especially under the glare of such a large operation. By the end of the day, all 81 men were back together, waiting to be picked up from this one spot. The Germans and Ustashi were not their only headaches. The Chetniks under General Mihajlovic, although not as formidable an underground organization as their rival Partisans, were still a force to contend with in early 1944.

The Partisans and Chetniks were ready and willing to risk their own lives in order to save as many downed Allied airmen as possible. However, whenever these rivals met face to face, there was always a fight to the death. Neither side was willing to end the civil war because of the power struggle to form the next government of Yugoslavia after the Germans were defeated.

As Germany's fate became more certain in the final two years of the war, the domestic rivalry in Yugoslavia only intensified. Many downed American flyers found themselves caught in the middle of this ugly game, as each side sought to eliminate the other.

The airfield in Bosan Petervac was the marshalling area for Allied airdrops to the Partisans at night. Its strategic location was vital for the distribution of food, arms, clothing and ammunition throughout the Balkans. Only in extreme circumstances, where wounded Partisans or downed flyers had to be flown back to Allied lines, would pilots run the risk of actually landing.

At first light the following morning, the snappish wail of distant engines broke the silence of the sleeping village. An anguished frown crept across Joe's drawn face as he forced his eyes open. "Christ! They're back!" he cursed to himself. Half dazed, he and about a dozen other men consigned to a farmhouse at the edge of the village, scattered across the yard as a pair of Stukas came screaming in from the west. Joe looked wildly about for a nice deep hole to crawl into. The ground shook under his feet with every bomb, but they missed their mark. Joe had his adrenaline fix for the day. It became routine over the next several days.

"They knew where we were," shrugs Joe. "The question was not if, but when they would be back."

His answer came the very next morning. Two more Stukas blasted a few more craters in the field next to their farmhouse. Again, the village and the airstrip were spared. How long their luck would hold out was anybody's guess.

The group's spirits rose later that day with a rumor that a C-47 might

A typical Partisan airstrip where wounded Partisans and Allied airmen were evacuated to American bases in Italy.

make it in that night. Joe didn't know whether to laugh or cry at that point. He was more preoccupied with his feet. One of the Partisan medics suspected gangrene was setting in. Joe needed to get to a hospital right away and was now on top priority for immediate evacuation. By now he could hardly walk.

That night, a band of Partisans and airmen walked to the airfield in high hopes. The stars were shining and there was no wind to speak of. Almost perfect conditions for a rescue. They had some oil soaked rags at the ready to mark the grassy runway. Just before midnight, a deep rumbling noise pierced the anxious silence. It was a plane. By the sound of it, it was getting closer by the minute. Anticipation grew to fever pitch. Then, parachutes were spotted in the distance. It was an airdrop. The engine noise faded into the darkness. No one said a word. Joe and his feet would have to wait.

The Stukas left their usual calling cards the next morning. Again, no real damage was done. Joe managed to hobble into a bomb crater from the day before, figuring the Germans couldn't hit the same spot twice. After the excitement of the early morning, the long wait for nightfall was on again. Patience, however, was getting short all around.

Card games could distract the men for only so long. Even Bill Kollar was losing interest in gambling. A real dangerous sign if there ever were one! And while the air raids were more of a nuisance than anything else,

Joe and the others had to wonder how much longer they could hold out before a full ground assault were launched against their tenuous hold on the airfield. As usual, no one told them a thing.

Friday, April 28. It was now twenty-six days since Joe and his crew had bailed out over Yugoslavia. Twenty-six long, hard days. Their morning started out a bit different for a change. No Stukas. No bombs. Just another endless day lay ahead before the next appointed hour. Surely there would be a plane tonight, they reasoned. Others besides Joe needed hospitalization for their injuries. Some had dysentery, including a few Partisans, while many were terribly malnourished. They all needed help in the worst way.

The daily call to Bari was made, with the usual promise that everything that could be done was being done on the other side of the Adriatic. Hopes began to rise with another setting sun. Just after dark, Joe was helped on to a horse cart for a bumpy ride to the landing strip. He could no longer walk on his own. Some of the sick and injured were piled in with him. The others ran or walked, determined more than ever to leave this godforsaken hellhole behind. Then they waited.

Midnight came and went. They strained to hear any sign of a plane. Nothing. Not a single solitary thing was out there except for a bank of fog they could see drifting down from the mountains. Another bitter disappointment! Then, the distant hum of airplane engines. Excitement exploded as everyone hurried to the edge of the airstrip. Joe was carried the last few yards on a stretcher. He felt a little foolish because of all the attention, but no one seemed to notice. The plane, still invisible in a sea of fog, was coming closer. It began to circle. It was overhead. One of the Partisans gave the nod and the oil rags were lit. A makeshift runway shimmered against the pitch black sky.

"By now we were going completely nuts," says Joe, "straining our eyes for any sign of the plane."

Some of the men broke down and sobbed like children. The strain was just too much. Joe had a puzzled look on his face as he tried to assess the situation. It just didn't make sense to him that any pilot in his right mind would try to land in such heavy fog, especially after so many clear nights had come and gone without a hint of a rescue. Was this for real? Was it really one of theirs somewhere out there in the murky beyond, or could this be a sneak attack? It troubled him that the Germans hadn't come calling that morning. Had they simply changed their timetable? Joe tried to shrug off his lingering doubts. If he thought about it any more he would go bonkers.

The noise from the engines indicated the plane was making its final approach. Visibility was still practically zero. Everybody held their breath. Everybody. Still, no plane in sight. Seconds that seemed like hours, crept by. Then, a phantom like shadow loomed up over the end of the grassy field. Lights appeared. Landing lights! And wings!

138

"It's one of ours!" someone thundered. "It's a C-47!" another chimed in.

The roar of the engines drowned out a chorus of tears and cheers as the plane bounced and then rolled to a stop. In the eerie glow of the burning oil rags, the zombie like men sprung to life, slapping each other on the back and hugging those who had made this all possible, the Partisan guides.

Watching from the sidelines, Joe didn't realize until that moment just how sweet freedom could taste. Tears filled his eyes as he paused to say a prayer of thanks.

There was no time to waste. The enemy was not far off. The side cargo door flung open. Without a word, every able-bodied man formed a line. There were supplies to be off-loaded. C-47s never came in empty handed, even on a mercy mission. The pilot kept his engines running just in case. Every second counted.

"My biggest fear," says Joe, "was that the Germans were still going to attack us then and there, since they hadn't shown up in the morning."

Allied airmen delivering supplies and picking up Allied airmen in Slovenija in a C-47 airplane. Joe was evacuated in a plane like this.

A C-47 (DC-3) loading wounded partisans and airmen at secret airstrip.

Within minutes the plane was empty. It was time to go. Twenty-six men crammed into the hollow belly of the aircraft. Then came the stretcher cases. Joe, still barely able to hobble on his own, was one of the last to board.

As he stood in the doorway, he turned and stared into a sea of uplifted faces. The rest of his shipmates, the other airmen and POWs and, of course, the Partisans who he owed his life to were silent. A lump welled up in his throat. Words wouldn't come. He could only manage a feeble smile. Then a hand reached out.

"See you back in Italy" John Reilly shouted over the roar of the revving engines as he shook his buddy's hand.

"You know Joe," he added with a sheepish grin, "I'm finally having a good day!"

Epilogue

1944-1997

Hitler built a fortress around Europe but he forgot to put a roof on it.
Franklin Delano Roosevelt

Joe Maloney

After a happy but uneventful two hour flight across the Adriatic Sea to the 15th USAAF Headquarters in Bari, Italy, Joe was rushed to the 26th Army General Hospital. Luckily, his feet were only badly infected. There was no gangrene, although the doctors told him it would have been a different story had he not been rescued when he was. His bandages had to be changed every four hours for the first few days until the infection started to drain and his feet began to heal. It was all very painful but, somehow, he got through it.

Joe lost 25 pounds during his ordeal and was so malnourished that he had a lot of trouble keeping food down. It was so bad that he had to be fed only small amounts every couple of hours, 24 hours a day, until he was able to regain some of his weight and strength. After about two weeks, he was released from hospital, although far from a picture of health.

Meanwhile, the rest of his crew made it back to Italy on the night of May 1 when enough planes were able to land to get everyone out at once. The next day, dozens of heavily armed German paratroopers stormed the village of Bosan Petrovac and executed everyone in sight.

Joe was debriefed by Army Intelligence in Bari and issued travel orders to return to the United States. He also received his pay of $144 for the month he had been absent. It figured out to the princely sum of $4.00 a day. U.S. military policy did not allow for repatriated airmen to be returned to active duty, at least not in the same theatre. If Joe were shot down again and captured, and the Germans found out it was his second time, he would be shot as a spy. His flying days were over. Joe wrote home to announce that reports of his presumed death were greatly exaggerated. It was good he did. The Army didn't get around to sending the official word of his rescue until a week after his letter arrived in Norfolk.

Joe's travel orders were open ended, which meant he could return to the States by any means he could, by sea or by air, as long as he made his own arrangements along the way. The Army, he was told in no uncertain terms, was no travel agency. After nearly dying for his country, he was on his own. Go figure.

All Allied military transportation was in utter chaos by this time. Unbeknownst to USAAF Headquarters in Bari, the cross channel invasion of Normandy was only a month away and most modes of transport, especially sea transport of all shapes and sizes, were at a premium. Joe would have to go by air. Considering his ordeal on the troopship just to get to the war, he felt himself lucky this time around.

A couple of days before he was ready to ship out, Joe had a visitor with an interpreter in tow. At first he didn't recognize the clean shaven face, but, then it dawned on him. It was the Frenchman nobody had trusted during the escape. His name, the man said, was Francis Richard, and he wanted to set the record straight. He explained that he had been in the French Navy but had been captured shortly after Germany launched its offensive against France and the Low Countries in May 1940. He later escaped only to be captured again. He escaped a second time, making his way through Germany and Austria and finally to Yugoslavia, where he met up with the Partisans. With tears in his eyes, Joe's visitor said he knew nobody trusted him but there was nothing he could do about the situation because of the language problem. When he kissed Joe on both cheeks to say good-bye, Francis Richard cried like a baby. So did Joe.

On the morning of May 8, Joe was reunited with two of his crewmates, Art Fleming and Bill Kollar, who were also trying to make their own arrangements to get back home. The trio decided to catch the first available flight to Lecce. When they arrived later that same afternoon, they were the first ones from their outfit to ever return after being shot down. Understandably, it caused quite a stir.

Ground Crew Chief Reinie Schweitzer thought he was seeing ghosts and pinched, poked and prodded Joe just to make sure he really was who he said he was. They had a lot of stories to catch up on since that fateful Palm Sunday. Joe sought out his old tent but it was already occupied by another crew. All his personal belongings were missing. The extra clothing he didn't care about, but it bothered him that all of his letters and photos from home were gone, along with his pistol and cache of wine. They were stolen, he was informed, by someone who probably thought he was never coming back. Nothing personal, he was reassured. It was just the way it was.

To add insult to injury, the base commander ordered Joe to sign a statement of loss for his aircraft. Uncle Sam had *Maggie's Drawers* listed at a value of $235,000. Joe wondered whether the government intended to collect. With a shrug of his shoulders, he signed anyway.

After two days in Lecce, the threesome caught a flight on a C-47 full of cargo and other servicemen, first to Sicily, then to Algeria and Casablanca. In Casablanca they had a two day layover. The base was crowded so Joe, Art and Bill were sent to the Red Cross hospice across town. Every bed was taken so they had to settle for some pillows and blankets on the hard, wet floor of the shower stalls. Nice welcome for returning heroes.

A few days later they were off to the Azores for a quick refueling stop before heading west across the Atlantic. There was another pit stop in Newfoundland before their plane touched down at Air Transport Command at LaGuardia Field in Long Island, New York. It was May 17. There was no marching band to greet them. Not even an official welcome. No matter. Joe was overjoyed to be home just the same.

Joe, Art and Bill shook hands and said good-bye before going their separate ways. Joe had 30 days of leave coming up with an expense account of a dollar a day and three cents a mile to help him enjoy it. Before catching the first train to Hartford, Connecticut, he called home with the news of his arrival. His mother and step-father were standing on the platform when he stepped off the train. Throwing his arms around his tearful mother, he knew he was home at last.

Back in Norfolk, Joe was heartbroken to learn of the death of his best friend, Jackie Mahoney, the guy he had peed in a bottle for on the day they enlisted. Serving with the Mighty 8th in Norwich, England, Jackie was shot down in April 1944, the same month as Joe, while on a one thousand plane bombing raid to Hamm, Germany. Filling the post of flight engineer on a B-17, it was to be his first and last mission.

Jackie managed to parachute to the German occupied town of Ingooigent in Belgium along with another crew member, James Cockriel. Hidden by the villagers, they considered trying to get back to England through France and Spain but the Belgium spy network advised against it. The border between France and Spain was too heavily guarded. Instead, the two flyers joined the Belgium Underground. While on patrol one night, they, along with several villagers, were surrounded and captured by a large German patrol following a short battle.

The prisoners were lined up against a ditch and shot. James survived his wounds but Jackie took a bullet through the head. He was buried in the village cemetery. He was 21, same age as Joe. Ingooigem was liberated by the British the very next morning.

After his leave was up, Joe reported to the Army base in Atlantic City. From there he was posted to the Don Cesar Hotel in St. Petersburg, Florida where he and other returning soldiers were encouraged to "talk out" their trauma with a staff psychiatrist. Joe was given sodium pentothal to help him remember his experiences. He felt like a guinea pig for the Army's new truth serum, but he went along with it anyway. There was always a party to go to somewhere in the hotel, so life wasn't so bad, everything considered. After six weeks of "treatment," Joe was sent to Miami Beach to await reassignment to active duty. It was there that he was told he might be shipped out as a tail gunner to the Pacific Theatre. "No way" was the way he put it to the army bigwigs. That was the last he ever heard of that.

The Charleston Air Base in South Carolina was his next home. Shortly after arriving, he almost lost his life in a car accident. Falling asleep at the wheel one night, he hit the abutment of a concrete bridge and the bridge won. The car careened down a steep embankment leaving him unconscious. It was some time before he came to and managed to crawl back up to the road side to flag down a passing truck. He was hospitalized in Maryland for the next two months with a fractured skull. He finished out the war, and then the rest of his military service, as a shipping clerk at the Charleston base.

On October 31, 1945, Joe was honorably discharged from the USAAC with the rank of Staff Sergeant at Westover Air Base near Springfield, Massachusetts. His military record noted he had a total of two years, three months and ten days in the service of his country. That didn't matter to Joe. He was just glad to be alive.

Joe was formally discharged from the army on the same day as his old friend Sam Tierney. In fact, they ran into each other for the first time since going overseas at the discharge office. Sam had also ended up serving on the air side as a fighter pilot. He too had been shot down but, unlike Joe, was captured and ended up as a POW for several years. Joe and Sam quickly rekindled their friendship, vowing never again to raid any rose gardens.

Joe earned the Purple Heart for wounds received in action (shrapnel in the leg), the Air Medal for shooting down an enemy plane, and an Oak Leaf Cluster for the danger of the Steyr mission, in addition to the European Theatre of War Medal and Good Conduct Medal. He also received two civilian awards, the Caterpillar Club Pin for making an emergency parachute jump (and living to tell about it), and the U.S. Late Arrivals Club Pin for making it back after being shot down over enemy territory.

Meanwhile, Joe had made a simple but very important vow to himself. Never again would he pick up a gun. He knew only too well what it felt like to be hunted down like an animal. There were to be no more hunting trips in the kaleidoscope of a Connecticut autumn. Ever. To this day he has kept his promise.

With no job to go to back in civilian life, Joe had no other choice but to move in with his mother, stepfather and grandmother. He survived on $20 a week, a form of unemployment insurance for war vets. The money didn't go very far, so, by Spring 1946, he got a job as a carpenter-apprentice under the GI Training Bill. Then he met Flora-Ann Menser. It was love at first sight. They were married April 7, 1947. Like his parents after the

Flora Ann and Joe Maloney, April 7, 1947.

Great War, it was time for Joe Maloney to get on with living, and that's what he did.

He returned to his former job in the experimental department at Pratt & Whitney Aircraft Corporation in East Hartford to support his young wife. In 1952 he decided to go into general contracting on his own, with nothing more than his last week's wages of $78 in his pocket.

Through sheer determination and a lot of hard work (and with Flora-Ann running the office), Joe was soon able to hire a few carpenters, and then a few more. His business quickly flourished. His customers ranged from families of modest means like his own, to bankers, doctors, lawyers and stockbrokers. He also worked at times with some of the finest architects from New York, Boston and Philadelphia. His penchant for building large reproduction homes throughout New England caught the eye of the *New York Times*, *America Home*, and *Life* magazines, which featured his work.

Later Joe became a licensed real estate broker and appraiser to better support his growing family. Michael (born February 1, 1948, died December 25, 1977) and Jody (born April 14, 1951). After 21 years in business, Joe and Flora-Ann decided it was time to retire. On November 6, 1973 they moved to Yarmouth County, Nova Scotia and became Canadian citizens on August 7, 1985. It would turn out to be a fateful move, one which would eventually take Joe back to his war years.

For 46 long years, Joe remained in the dark about many of the details of his escape in Yugoslavia. All this changed on March 17, 1990, when he was invited to a St. Patrick's Day party at the home of a friend in Yarmouth, Dr. Shelagh Leahey. That's where he met Ana Brodarec. A resident of Zagreb, Croatia, she was visiting her son, Ivo, a local doctor.

145

Ana Brodarec had been a Partisan during the war. As a 19-year-old member of the Progressive Student Underground, and while still a freshman at the Institute of Technology in Zagreb, she participated in a mass uprising against the German occupation forces. Leaving Zagreb in 1941 to become a full-time member of the Partisans, after it became too dangerous for her to remain in the capital, she and her medical student husband helped to organize and deliver medical care to the underground. They were instrumental in setting up Partisan field hospitals all over Croatia.

Joe told Ana as much as he could remember about the mountains and villages he had seen so long ago. After several discussions, Ana slowly started to put the pieces together. As soon as she returned home to Croatia, she contacted Edi Selhaus, another former Partisan living in Ljubljana, Slovenija. A well known author and photographer, he had written a book "Stotinka Srece" (Lucky Chance), a collection of war stories about United States airmen who had been shot down over Slovenija and saved by the Partisans. The names of Joe and his crew were already listed in his book.

Comparing notes, along with the help of old Partisan maps and records, Edi Selhaus and Ana Brodarec managed to fill in the rest of the blanks. There was only one thing left for Joe to do to complete the picture. After nearly half a century, he would have to go back to Yugoslavia.

In September 1993, he and Flora-Ann (along with the author) flew to Slovenija to meet Edi Selhaus and another local author on Partisan activities, Janez Zerovc. They began to look for anybody who might have helped Joe and his crew in 1944. They were not to be disappointed.

Ana Brodarec and Joe Maloney with plaque Joe made and sent to the Partisans September 1992 for their exhibition to thank them for saving his crew during April of 1944.

146

The village well that Joe recognized from 50 years ago in Podgrad brought back a lot of memories.

With the help of Edi and Janez, along with former Partisan, Stanislav Erjavec, Joe was able to retrace some of the steps he had taken a half century earlier. He returned to Podgrad where it had all begun on April 2, 1944. Like his first time there, a crowd soon gathered as he walked into the still rustic but beautiful village. They wanted to get a first hand look at their returning hero.

At first Joe didn't recognize a thing. After all, it had been so long ago and in very different circumstances. He took Flora-Ann aside and whispered the disheartening news that he had never been to this place before. He wrung his hands over how he was going to break the news to his gracious hosts. He was embarrassed because a civic luncheon was about to be held in his honor.

Joe needed to collect his thoughts. He slipped away from the crowd and began to walk up a steep hill to the center of the village. There, finally, it all came back to him. He recognized the church, and the rectory next door, where he had stayed that first night. And, he remembered the old well by the side of the road. Yes, this is where he had spent his 21st birthday!

Regaining his confidence, Joe waded back into the crowd to meet the daughter of Janez Ambrozic, the man who had first told him and his crew about the Partisans; the man who had pleaded with them not to know the names of any person or village along the escape route. Joe offered a prayer at Janez's grave in the church courtyard. He talked to several people who had lived through the air assault on Podgrad the day after his crew had slipped away. Joe and the people of Podgrad basked in the warmth of their new friendship. He was the first downed American airman to ever return to their area.

Joe also visited the site where his plane had crashed in Tolsti vrh, a luscious highside vineyard in 1993. The trunk of a nearby Cherry tree still displayed the black scars from the fire when *Maggie's Drawers* drilled herself into her grave. There, Joe met Anton Kos who had stood on that very same spot as a young boy in 1944. Anton presented him with a piece of his bomber, a piston valve taken from the engine that he and his friends had carted away. Through an interpreter, Anton told Joe that he had been saving two piston valves in the hope that, someday, one of the crewmen might return to take one of his souvenirs back home. He insisted on keeping the other part for himself as a symbol of their shared past.

Anton's wife, Antonija, had also seen Joe's plane fall from the sky back in 1944. In 1993, she described in arm waving detail how his plane swooped down over her house with a trail of smoke (gasoline vapor) before disappearing from view. She told Joe through an interpreter that she was surprised that the Germans and the White Guard didn't shoot the airmen in their parachutes. She also related the story of how the Partisans had to burn her house down a few months later in order to keep the enemy from capturing it.

Joe later shared a glass of Slivovitz with 84 year old Franciska Sparovec on the same bench where three of his crewmates had stopped to rest after bailing out. Joe wondered whether the booze tasted just as good to his shipmates back then. Franciska never thought she would live to see the day when one of her "handsome fly boys" would come back.

Joe was also warmly received in Novo Mesto, the former Nazi stronghold, by Mayor Franci Koncilija, who presented him with a hand carved commemorative plaque on behalf of a thankful city. Inscribed on the plaque were two dates: 4-2-1944 and 9-2-1993, the day he was shot down; and the day he returned to Slovenija. Novo Mesto is a city that never forgot.

At the Novo Mesto Museum, Joe met Franc Brulc, the man who had saved Fred Streicher. With a twinkle in his eye, Franc asked Joe whether Fred still had his beautiful watch. And, to his complete astonishment, Joe was introduced to Marija Klobucar, the young lady who had "welcomed" him to Yugoslavia the first time with a pitch fork. On their second encounter, they exchanged warm smiles and kisses instead. And, yes, Marija had made a beautiful blouse out of Joe's parachute.

Over the next several days, Joe was guided back to the banks of the Kopa River where he and the other escapees had been taken across in a rowboat, three at a time. He later met Stanko Kusljan who gave him a machine gun part from *Maggie's Drawers*. A friend of Stanko's had been saving it for such an occasion. At the Museum of Modern History in Ljubljana, curator Matija Zgajnar presented Joe with a spoon, made from the melted down parts of the downed B-24 by the Partisans.

Joe had collected quite a few souvenirs, thanks to the generosity of his hosts. Unfortunately, he didn't get to take all the hardware back home with him. Heavily armed security guards at the Leonardo da Vinci Airport in Rome wouldn't let him through with his machine gun part for a connecting flight to Canada. He had no choice but to leave his piece of treasure behind. And, he had one other disappointment.

The night before he was scheduled to leave Slovenija, he met a man by the name of Kuret Dusan in the lobby of the Grand Union Hotel in Ljubljana. Through an interpreter, Dusan explained that an official German report on the crash of his plane and his crew's escape had been written in 1944. Joe, of course, was intrigued.

Dusan further informed a very elated Joe that he had seen the original German file hidden among some old government records in Belgrade and that his brother would try to retrieve a copy. However, in the wake of the breakup of Yugoslavia, it is unlikely the German report will ever surface again. Joe will likely never know what his enemies had to say about him and his crew in April 1944. It probably wasn't very complimentary, but he would love to know just the same.

Joe will be forever grateful to Ana Brodarec for leading him to his path of rediscovery. For Ana, the feeling of admiration is mutual because of their shared wartime experiences. So much so, that she has presented him with a very special badge. A note written on that occasion explains it all: "On the 6/22/1941, near Sisak, the town in Croatia, in the forest and below the big elm, was founded the first Partisan squad in Europe. This squad was the nucleus of the Liberation Army, and, with the Allies, was the winner in the World War II battles against Germany. I was a member of this first squad, and this badge was given to me as a remembrance of this event. Now, this badge is my gift to you, Joe, my dear friend and comrade from the World War II."

Joe and Flora-Ann continue to live in Yarmouth, Nova Scotia. They keep in touch with their new friends in Slovenija and hope to return some day. Their bond is unbreakable. A day never goes by that Joe does not give thanks to the brave Partisans who helped save his life and those of his crew. He constantly remembers them in his prayers.

Joe Maloney flanked by Matija Zgajnar, curator of the Ljubljana Museum of Modern History (right of photo) and Edi Selhaus, former Partisan and author. Edi was instrumental in helping Joe retrace his war years half a century after he was shot down.

Fred Streicher

Three days after being wounded, Streicher found himself in a German field hospital. The place was nothing more than a barn meant for meatball surgery. Gangrene had already set in his leg, so, an amputation, guillotine style, was performed below the knee without an anesthetic. Just before the procedure was carried out, Streicher asked the doctor if there were any other way to save his leg. As a prisoner of war it occurred to him he might not have the best health plan.

"First I am a doctor, then I am a German," came the reassuring reply.

A few days later Streicher barely survived a bombing raid by the Allies. It happened at a railroad station where he had been en route to another prison camp. A lot of civilians were killed and the crowd turned ugly. The guards had to rush Fred and several other wounded American soldiers from the platform to the basement of the station to avoid a lynching on the spot.

Streicher was later transferred to a full German military hospital in Zagreb before being admitted to yet another hospital, this time in Prague, to recover. Months later, he was sent to Obermassfeld, Germany, where his leg was reamputated through the mid-thigh because of recurring infection. The procedure was done at a POW hospital on October 10, 1944, by an English doctor. The operation almost killed him. A young German soldier volunteered to give him blood, a gesture that probably saved his life.

During his time as a POW, Streicher was in constant pain from his amputations. He received little medical attention but managed to survive with the help of Red Cross packages from home.

On January 22, 1945, Streicher was repatriated. His return to the States aboard the Red Cross ship *M.S. Gripsholm* marked the last exchange of wounded POWs to be completed between Germany and the United States before the end of the war. He disembarked in New York to a military band playing the tune *Don't Fence Me In*. The attempt at humor did not escape him. Despite his condition, he still had a quick laugh.

Streicher spent the next six months at Walter Reed General Hospital in Washington, DC where he underwent another operation due to infolding of scar tissue and drainage needed on his

A boy's school in Germany where Joe's pilot, Fred Streicher was a POW, 1944-1945.

amputated leg. He was fitted with a prosthesis in August 1945 and slowly eased back into active duty.

In January 1946, Streicher retired from the military with the rank of Captain and returned to the University of Pittsburgh to earn a degree in electrical engineering. He joined a large company that did business all over Pennsylvania. In the following year he married his high school sweetheart and started a family.

Streicher lived an active life despite constant pain from his stump. Besides his demanding job, he water skied, hunted and fished and often returned to his first love, flying small airplanes. He retired in 1969 after suffering a stroke, spending the last year of his life in a wheelchair.

Fred Streicher died of pneumonia at his home in Bethel Park, Pennsylvania on October 23, 1989. Never bitter with the hand the war had dealt him, he always had the same reply whenever asked about his wooden leg: "I zigged when I should have zagged." His widow Eileen keeps in touch with Joe and Flora-Ann.

Ed Brady

Bailing out of *Black Magic* over Regeensburg, Bavaria on February 22, 1944, Joe's first pilot survived to become POW #2781 in Germany for the rest of the war. Seven months after being shot down, he heard what had happened to *Maggie's Drawers* from some of the new prisoners. He constantly worried about his old crew, not knowing whether they had lived or died.

From his letters to his sister, it appears Brady was treated reasonably well by his captors. However, he depended heavily on Red Cross packages to survive as there was always a shortage of food, such as it was, especially in the last months of the war. The Russians liberated his prison camp in May 1945 and, after being turned over to the Americans, he was shipped home to Victoria, Texas.

Within weeks of his repatriation, he married and quit the service as a Second Lieutenant. Years later he re-enlisted with the Air Force but at a lower rank. He served in Iwo Jima, Germany and England before committing suicide on December 8, 1963. Following an investigation, the military ruled Ed Brady's untimely death service related.

Clark Fetterman

The bombardier chose to stay in the Air Force after the war and retired a Lieutenant Colonel in 1983. He died in 1985 in Arlington, Virginia, his prized autograph of Shirley Temple still among his prized possessions.

William Birchfield

The navigator settled down in Little Rock, Arkansas after the war. He died December 10, 1992. In the fall of 1992, Joe managed to track him down for the first time since the war. However, Birchfield, still the loner, refused to meet with Joe or discuss anything with him about their wartime experiences.

Clarence Jensen
The flight engineer from Fresno, California stayed in the service after the war. He was killed in the crash of a B-24 while flying as an instructor off the coast of California in 1947. He was 27.

John Reilly
The radio operator and top turret gunner resigned from the service after coming home from the war and later became a motorcycle cop in New York City. Since then, Joe lost all contact with his buddy who was always trying to have a "good day."

Arthur Fleming
The ball gunner still lives in Clairton, near Pittsburgh, where he is retired from a steel mill.
Art and Joe met for the first time since the war in September 1992 in Pittsburgh. Reluctant to talk about the war, Art Fleming insisted "that was then and this is now." He is the only other crewmember from *Maggie's Drawers* known to be alive today.

William Kollar
All attempts to locate the waist gunner have failed.

Ed O'Connor
The nose gunner worked as a part-time tour guide at the Grand Ole Opry in his hometown of Nashville, Tennessee after he retired to civilian life. He died of cancer on October 2, 1992, the day before Joe had arranged to meet him in Nashville. They had been in touch by phone a month earlier when Ed promised to stay alive long enough to see his old war buddy. Unfortunately, their reunion was not to be.

Waldo Akers
All attempts to locate the waist gunner have failed.

Reinee Schweitzer
The ground crew chief for *Maggie's Drawers* returned to the United States in 1944 and was stationed at Gowen Field, Boise, Idaho. Discharged in 1945, he worked for the United States Postal Service until 1978. He was then employed by Idaho Law Enforcement until 1983. Schweitzer retired in Boise, where he died July 12, 1998.

Newbold Noyes Jr.

The cub reporter from *Little Joe* went on to become the editor of the *Washington Star*. Now retired, he lives with his wife in Sorrento, Maine. In March, 1994, Joe contacted him by letter through another veteran living in New England. Shortly before noon, on April 2, 1994, Noyes telephoned Joe and they spoke for the first time, exactly 50 years to the day and to the hour, after Joe's plane was shot down. They met briefly in Maine in the Fall of 1994 to talk about old times.

98th Bombardment Group

The 98th was redeployed to the United States after V-E Day with a total of 417 combat missions to its credit. The Group was ordered to stand-by for additional training to enter the Pacific Theatre, but the surrender of Japan in August 1945 made this unnecessary.

The 98th was deactivated as a Bombardment Group on November 10, 1945. It was reactivated July 1, 1947 and redesignated the 98th Bombardment Wing on July 12, 1948. It entered the Korean Conflict in 1950 flying B-29s. The 98th Strategic Wing, the Bombardment Wing's successor, was deactivated December 31, 1976, bringing to an end more than 30 years of stellar military service.

The 98th returned to live again as the 98th Air Refueling Group on May 12, 1987. It has since been called into active duty in two war zones. In 1989, it flew during *Operation Just Cause*, the United States invasion of Panama. In 1990, it flew in support of the multi-national force in *Desert Storm,* the Gulf War.

The Partisans: Stanislav Erjavec

The Intelligence Officer who saved one of Joe's crew became a law enforcement officer after the war. After retiring, he owned a very success- ful herbal medicine company. He died at his home in Ljubljana in July 1995.

Franc Planic/Milan Zagorc/Franc Brulc

They are living in the Ljubljana area and met Joe when he returned to Slovenija in 1993. Franc Planic is a retired Colonel in the Yugoslav army. Milan Zagorc is a retired Lieutenant Colonel. Franc Brulc retired as Com- mander of the National Safeguard Unit.

William Jones

Having completed his mission to Yugoslavia in June 1944, Mayor Jones flew to Bari, Italy and then to Algiers to prepare his official report on the Partisans for the Allies. His complete findings were published two years later under the title *Twelve months with Tito's Partisans*.

He returned to England a hero in July 1944 and immediately went on a lecture tour throughout the British Isles, always keeping secret the names of the people and places he had come into contact with. Shortly after, Major Jones went home to Canada to more public appearances and newspaper interviews about his exploits in Yugoslavia.

He and his wife Helen eventually settled on a farm in Ontario on the Niagara Peninsula. Major Jones promptly named it *Belgrade Farm* in honor of the Partisans. In return, Marshal Tito renamed a street in Belgrade *Jones Avenue.* Over the years, Jones returned several times to Yugoslavia at the personal invitation of President Tito to receive a number of national honors and awards. Although he continued to speak publicly about his wartime experiences, his full story could not be told until the veil of government secrecy was lifted after 30 years in 1973.

On the morning of August 25, 1969, Major Jones collapsed while working in his barn. He died September 1, at Belgrade Farm in Wellandport, Ontario. He was 74. Dr. Tode Curuvija, the Yugoslav ambassador to Canada, delivered the eulogy at his funeral. The intrepid Major Jones took his wartime secrets to his grave.

BIBLIOGRAPHY

Primary Unpublished Manuscripts

1. *Allied Airmen and Prisoners of War Rescued by the Slovene Partisans*. Research Institute of Ljubljana, 1946.

2. Casualty Information Report for the Adjutant General's Office. AAF, Atlantic City, New Jersey, 17 July 1944.

3. Casualty Information Report for the Adjutant General's Office. AAF Redistribution Station. Miami Beach, Florida, 9 June 1944.

4. Combat Equipment Lost Report. 415th Bombardment Squadron (H) Air Corps. Office of the Armament Officer, New York, 3 April 1944.

5. *El Alamein to Allemagne-History of the 98th Bomb Group*, 28 March 1944.

6. General Orders No. 200. Awards of the Air Medal. HQ 15th Air Force. APO520, 11 April 1944.

7. General Orders No. 39. HQ Ninth Air Force, APO 520. New York, 6 May 1944.

8. General Orders No. 39. HQ Ninth Air Force. APO 696, U.S. Army, 25 February 1944.

9. Individual Casualty Questionnaire. File No. 3880, 2 April 1946.

10. Individual Flight Record. 98th Bomb (H) 415th Bomb (H). Enlisted Men-Heavier Than Air: January 1944; February 1944; March 1944.

11. Letters from Ed Brady. 26 December 1943; 24 January 1944.

12. Memorandum. Headquarters 47th Wing. U.S. Army. 30 March 1944.

13. National Military Records. National Archives and Records Administration. St. Louis, Mo.

14. Report of Disinterment and Reburial. Co.M. 102nd Infantry. 24 August 1921.

15. *Short Saga of a Replacement Crew.*,15th Air Force, 98th Bomb Group, 344th Squadron. Ploesti, 24 June 1944.

16. Special Narrative Report No. 23. 98th Bombardment Group (H) AC, APO 520, U.S. Army, 2 April 1944.

17. Statement on Missing Crew. 415th Bombardment Squadron (H) AAF New York, 3 April 1944.

18. Transmittal of Missing Air Crew Report. 98th Bombardment Group (H) AC. Office of the Group commander, 9 April 1944.

19. War Department. Graves Registration Service. American Expeditionary Forces. 29 March 1918.

20. War Diary. HQ 98th Bomb Group (H) AC, 1 January-1 February 1944 (Manduria, Italy); 1 February-1 March 1944 (Lecce, Italy);1 March-1 April 1944 (Lecce, Italy).

NEWSPAPERS

Atlantic Advocate (Halifax, Nova Scotia) 1970
Chronicle Herald (Halifax, Nova Scotia) 1980
Digby Courier (Nova Scotia) 1968
Dolenski List (Novo Mesto, Slovenija) 1993
Hamilton Spectator (Ontario) 1968
Hardford Courant (Connecticut) 1985
MacLeans (Toronto) 1994
Mail Star (Halifax, Nova Scotia) 1987
New York Times 1929
Poway News Chieftain (Connecticut) 1994
Register Citizen (Winsted, Connecticut) 1985
Springfield Republican (Massachusetts) 1918
Steyrer Zeitung (Austria) 1964
Svobodna Misel (Slovenija) 1993
Sunday Star (Washington D.C.) 1944
Waterbury Republican (Connecticut) 1945
Winsted Evening Citizen (Connecticut) 1923, 1944, 1991
The Vanguard (Yarmouth, Nova Scotia) 1990, 1992, 1995

PUBLISHED SOURCES

AAF. *B-24:The Liberator-Pilot Training Manual*. Cleveland, Ohio: Copifyer Lithograph Corp., 1944.

Angelucci, E.; Matricardi, P. *Combat Aircraft of World War II 1941-1942*. New York: Military Press, 1988.

Ardery, Philip. *Bomber Pilot-A Memoir of World War II*. Lexington, Ky.: University Press of Kentucky, 1978.

Baruch, Bernard M. *American Industry in the War-A Report of the War Industries Board*. New York: Prentice-Hall, Inc., 1941.

Beer, Siegfried; Karner, Stefan. *Der Krieg aus der Luft*. Karnten und Stiermark 1941-1945. (Graz 1992).

Beck, Earl R. *Under the Bombs-The German Home Front 1942-1945*. Lexington, Ky.: University Press of Kentucky, 1986.

Birdsall, Steve. *Log of the Liberators*. New York: Doubleday & Company, Inc., 1973.

Caldwell, C. *Air Power and Total War*. New York: Coward-McCann, 1943.

Carigan, William. *Ad Lib:Flying the B-24 Liberator in World War II*. Manhattan, Kansas: Sunflower University Press, 1988.

Chant, Chris. *Air Forces of World War I & World War II*. London: Quarto Publishing Ltd., 1979.

Chant, C; Humble R.; Davis, J.F.; Macintyre, D.; Gunston B. *Air Warfare*. New York: Thomas Y. Crowell Company, 1975.

Costello, John. *Love Sex & War-Changing Values 1939-45*. London: Collins, 1985.

Craven, W. E.; Cate, J. L. *The Army Air Forces in World War II, Vols. I, II, III*. Chicago: University of Chicago Press, 1948, 1949, 1951.

Dancocks, Daniel G. *Welcome to Flanders Fields*. Toronto: McClelland & Stewart, 1989.

Deighton, Len. *Fighter-The True Story Of The Battle of Britain*. London: Jonathan Cape Ltd., 1977.

Dunmore, Spencer; Carter, William. *Reap the Whirlwind: The Untold Story of 6 Group, Canada's Bomber Force of World War II*. Toronto: McClelland/Stewart, 1991.

Eells, Hastings. *Europe Since 1500*. New York: Henry Holt & Company, 1933.

Ethell, J.; Grinsell, R.; Freeman, R.; Anderton, D.; Johnsen, F.; Sweetman, B.; Vanags-Baginskis, A.; Mikesh, R. *The Great Book of World War II Airplanes*. Tokyo, New York: Bonanza Books, 1984.

Giesler, Patricia. *Valour Remembered-Canada and the First World War*. Ottawa: Department of Veterans Affairs, 1982.

Giesler, Patricia. *Valour Remembered-Canada and the Second World War*. Ottawa: Veterans Affairs Canada, 1981.

Gilbert, Martin. *Second World War*. Toronto: Stoddart, 1989.

Gwyn, Sandra. *Tapestry of War* Toronto: Harper Collins Publishers, 1992.

Haber, L. F. *The Poisonous Cloud-Chemical Warfare in the First World War*. New York: Oxford University Press, 1986.

Hastings, Max. *Bomber Command*. London: Micheal Joseph Limited, 1979.

Hoobler, D. & T. *The Trenches-Fighting on the Western Front in World War I* New York: Putnam, 1978.

Hurst, David A. *Force For Freedom-The Legacy of the 98th*. Paducah, Ky: Turner Publishing, 1990.

Hurst, David A. *Force For Freedom-The Legacy of the 98th. Vol.II*. Paducah, Ky: Turner Publishing, 1990.

Isabella Club. *Norfolk, Connecticut-The First Two Hundred years 1758-1958* Norfolk: Bicentennial Committee of Norfolk, Connecticut, 1958.

Jablonski, Edward. *Airwar-Outraged Skies*. New York: Doubleday, 1971.

Jablonski, Edward. *Airwar-Terror From The Sky*. New York: Doubleday, 1971.

Jane's *Fighting Aircraft of World War II*. London: Bracken Books, 1989.

Johnson, Frederick A. *Air Museum Journal-Liberator Lore, Vols. I, II, III, IV*. Tacoma, Washington: Museum Aeronautica, 1989.

Jones, Major William. *Twelve Months with Tito's Partisans*. Bedford, England: Bedford Books Limited, 1946.

Kennedy, Paul. *The Rise and Fall of the Great Powers*. London: Random House, 1988.

Lutz, Volker. *Bombenangriffe auf Steyr*. Steyr: Amtsblatt Der Stadt Steyr, 1985.

Maass, Peter. *Love Thy Neighbor*. New York: Alfred A. Knopf, 1996.

MacIsaac, David. *The United States Strategic Bombing Survey, Vols. III, IV*. New York: Garland Publishing, 1976.

MacLean, Fitzroy. *Tito*. Maidenhead, England: McGraw-Hill, 1980.

McKee, Alexander. *Dresden 1945-The Devil's Tinderbox*. New York: E.P. Dutton, Inc., 1982.

Military Affairs/Aerospace Historian. *The Development of the Heavy Bomber 1918-1944* USAF Historical Studies No. 6. Manhattan, Kansas

Morris, Eric; Chant, Christopher; Johnson, Curt; Willmott, H.P. *Weapons & Warfare of the 20th Century*. London: Octopus Books Limited, 1976.

Newby, Leroy W. *Into the Guns of Ploesti*. Osceola, WI: Motorbooks International, 1991.

Norfolk Historical Society Bicentennial Committee. *Our Town-Norfolk, Connecticut, 1975*.

Peden, Murray. *A Thousand Shall Fall*. Stittsville, Ontario: Canada's Wings, 1979.

Reader's Digest Ltd., *The World At Arms*, London: 1989.

Reyes, Gary. *Airplanes: Our Quest to Reach the Skies*. New York: Michael Friedman Publishing Group, 1990.

Roehm, A. Wesley; Buske, Morris R.; Webster, Hutton; Wesley, Edgar B. *The Record of Mankind*. Vancouver: Copp Clark Publishing, 1949, 1952.

Rys, Steven. *U.S. Military Power*. Greenwich, Ct: Bison Books, 1983.

Selhaus, Edi. *Evasion and Repatriation-Slovene Partisans and Rescued American Airmen in World War II*. Manhattan, Kansas: Sunflower University Press, 1993.

Selhaus, Edi. *Stotinka Srece*. Ljubljana, Slovenija: Zalozba Borec, 1980.

Shirer, William. *The Rise and Fall of the Third Reich*. New York: Simon & Schuster, 1960.

Simon & Schuster. *Encyclopedia of World War 11*. New York: Simon & Schuster, 1978.

Sims, Edward H. *The Aces Talk*. New York: Ballantine, 1972.

Steyr Walzlager Ges. m.b.h., *Steyr*, 1990.

Straight, Michael. *Make This The Last War-The Future of the United Nations*. New York: Harcourt, Brace & Company, 1943

Swing, Raymond Gram. *Preview of History*. New York: Doubleday, Doran and Company, Inc., 1943.

Tagg, Michael C. *Battle In The Air*. Surrey, England: Archive Publishing, 1990.

Taylor, John W.R. A H*istory of Aerial Warfare*. London: Hamlyn, 1974.

Toland, John. *Adolf Hitler*. New York: Ballantine Books, 1976.

Tuchman, Barbara, W. *The Guns of August*, New York: Bantan Books, 1962.

Ulrich, Johann. *Der Luftkrieg uber Osterreich 1939-1945*. Wien: Militarhistorische Schriftenreine, Heft 5/6, Lrsg. vom Heeresheschichtlichen Museum, 1967.

Verrier, Anthony. *The Bomber Offensive*. London: B.T. Batsford Ltd., 1968.

Waldecker, Alice V. *Norfolk, Connecticut-The First Two Hundred Years 1758-1958*. Norfolk: Bicentennial Committee of Norfolk, Connecticut, 1958.

Ward, Ray. *Those Brave Crews*. Bend, Oregon: Maverick Publications, 1989.

Welsh, George. *Briefing-Journal of the International B-24 Liberator Club*. San Diego: Skywood Press, 1994.

Westheimer, David. *Rider on the Wind*. New York: Pinnacle Books, 1979.

Wren, Jack. *The Great Battles of World War I*. London: Grosset & Dunlap, 1971.

Wyatt, Bernie. *Maximum Effort. The Big Bombing Raids*. Erin, Ontario: The Boston Mills Press, 1986.

Additional Thoughts

I would like to dedicate this book to the following:

To my grandmother, Minnie Bouchet, who raised me from early childhood until I entered the Service.

To my wife, Flora Ann for the true love and devotion throughout our fifty-one years of marriage. She has always encouraged and backed me in every way.

To the Partisans of Slovenija, Croatia, and Bosnia, who put their own lives at risk every day that we were there in 1944, to save us. Many died protecting us.

To Major William Jones, a British Intelligence Officer from Bear River, Nova Scotia. He worked with the Partisans to save my crew along with many other Allied airmen shot down during World War II.

To my new found friend Ray Zinck, who asked if he could write my story. He has worked tirelessly for the past several years to bring this book to completion.

And to God for watching over me and blessing me in every way, by bringing all the above people into my life to make it full and complete.

Joe Maloney
August 1998

Stanko Kusljan, far right, a Partisan gave Joe a piece of his airplane, Sept. 1993.

Joe touching tree where his plane crashed. The tree is still oozing pitch after 50 years. Joe's plane crashed in 1944 near the Village of Tolsti vrh. Photo taken September 1993.

Sept. 1, 1993, Joe and Stanko Kusljan giving Joe a part of his airplane that crashed April 2, 1944, Nagmajni, Slovenija.

161

September 1993, Joe overlooking area where plane flew before it crashed in 1944 at Tolsti vrh.

Joe overlooking Podgrad, Slovenija, Sept. 1, 1993. This is where he and his crew were taken by Partisans after jumping out of their B-24 in 1944.

Village of Gornja Tezka Voda, Slovenija where three members of Joe's crew were taken. The lady second from left is Franciska Sparovec who offered them food and drink, Sept. 1, 1993.

Joe, Maria Klobucar (first person Joe saw when he landed in Slovenija and he gave her his parachute), Franc Brulc(saved pilot Fred Streicker), and Stan Enjavec (Partisan who saw crew jump from the plane). Sept. 2, 1993.

Joe and Franciska Sparovec(age 84) in village of Garnja Tezka Voda, Sept. 1, 1993. On April 2, 1944, she sat on the same bench and offered goulash and wine to three of Joe's crew.

An aerial view of the village of Podgrad. Joe and crew stayed there April 2-3, 1944. Photo taken September 1993.

Catholic Church Rectory, Podgred, Slovenia, Regional Headquarters of Partisans during the war. Photo taken September 1993.

More than half a century later, Joe still has the "D" handle to the parachute he used on April 2, 1944.

Art Fleming, ball turret gunner and Joe Maloney, tail gunner at Fleming home, Clarion, PA., Oct. 2, 1992. Note difference in sizes of these two men.

Index

Numerical Listings

A

B

C

D

E

Eaker, Ira C. 68
Earle, Clifford 27
East Hartford 39, 86
Eastern Front 56
El Alamein 69
El Paso, Texas 20, 21
Erjavec, Stanislav 5, 95, 97, 111, 147, 153, 163

F

Fasig Jr., Henry 5
Ferguson, Frank 25
Ferron, Stefan 6
Fetterman, Clark 21, 42, 48, 49, 53, 77, 83, 88, 105, 130, 151
Fields, Cay 6
Fields, Harold 6
Fifth Corps Command 134
Fischer, Bob 44
Flak Jacket 59, 71, 86
Fleming, Art 5, 22, 42, 82, 87, 99, 105, 122, 128, 142, 152, 164
Flentje, Stan 5
"Flimsy" 49
Flying Boxcar 43
Flying Coffin 43
Flying Fortress 9, 43, 56, 74, 84
Foggia 32
Ford and Douglas 42
Fort Biggs 20
Fort Devens, Massachusetts 14, 16, 65
Fortunato Cesare Airdrome 34, 41
Fourth Battalion 95, 97, 111
France 25, 26, 35, 36, 46, 62
Franco-Prussian War 35
Fresno, California 22, 152
Fruhauf, Josef 86
FW-190 73, 79, 87

G

Gable, Clark 17
Garfield, John 64
General Staff 25
German Air Defense 74
German Sixth Offensive 134
Germany 9, 11, 12, 26, 28, 38, 55, 56, 71, 95, 122, 136, 142, 149, 150, 151
Gerstenberg, Alfred 91
GI Training Bill 145
Gilbert Clock Company 38
Gorjanci 95, 96, 97
Gornja Tezka Voda 98, 162
Gornje 110
Gotha Bomber 40
Gowen Field 152
Grand Island, Nebraska 20
Grand Union Hotel 149
Great Depression 10, 38, 60

Great War 8, 16, 26, 27, 35, 36, 37, 40, 56, 85, 108, 118, 145
Greece 70
Green, Truman 10
Grey, Edward 25
Gulf of Mexico 19

H

Haggerty, Paul 5
Hague Convention 27
Hamm, Germany 143
Harris, Jim 6
Hartford, Connecticut 15, 84, 143
Hitler, Adolf 11, 27, 41

I

IP (Initial Point) 48
Ireland 36
Isle of Capri 68
Italy 9, 10, 11, 12, 32, 39, 42, 46, 48, 61, 63, 70, 72, 88, 106, 110, 116, 125, 135, 140, 141
Iwo Jima 151

J

Jackman, Francis 63
James River 27
Japan 38, 39, 153
Jenkins, Terry 5
Jensen, Clarence 22, 42, 48, 70, 83, 87, 105, 152
Johnson, Gladys 5
Jones Avenue 154
Jones, William 117, 153
JU-52 134
Julian Alps 74
Junkers 88s 72
Jurna vas 97

K

K-rations 67
Karnes, William E. 33, 34
Klagenfurt 74
Klobucar, Marija 6, 163, 148
Knowles, Bruce 6
Kofler, Andrea 6
Kollar, William 22, 42, 65, 84, 87, 98, 113, 135, 137, 142, 152
Koncilija, Franci 6, 148
Kopa River 148
Korean Conflict 153
Kos, Anton 5, 6, 92, 100, 101, 148
Krvatska Palje 119
Kuhns, Paul 5
Kuret, Dusan 6
Kurner, Ray 5, 10, 32
Kusljan, Stanko 5, 148, 161

(From the original front cover flap)

The Final Flight
of Maggie's
Drawers

by Ray E. Zinck

The Final Flight of Maggie's Drawers is the true story of Joe Maloney, a B-24 tail gunner during World War II. After training, Joe was attached to the 15th Air Force, 415 Squadron based in southern Italy.

His story unfolds as he describes, in detail, life in the military, from living in a tent city to countless bombing runs over Nazi-held Europe.

Joe partakes in countless missions until one fateful day in 1944 during a bombing run to Steyr, Austria. Riddled with flak and bullets, Maggie's Drawers, his B-24, receives a fatal hit. Her crew is forced to bailout over Yugoslavia. The story unfolds as Joe's crewmates are reunited on the ground, and are led by Allied Partizans to the free-zone.

The race to freedom is dangerous, as they encounter Nazi patrols, German-held towns and Axis sympathizers, until they are finally airlifted back to Italy.

This is a gripping story of American boys trapped behind enemy lines, and a heroic group of locals who risked their lives to save them. Truly, this story should be told again and again.

Printed in the USA
CPSIA information can be obtained
at www.ICGtesting.com
JSHW082341140824
68134JS00020B/1816

9 781681 624013